Learning To Love Him By Trusting Him

Real Talk on Love, Letdowns, and Holding On

By Ce'ce Perez

First published by Sherila Perez 2025

Copyright © 2025 by Ce'Ce Perez

All rights reserved. No part of this publication may be reproduced, stored, or transmitted in any form or by any means, electronic, mechanical, photocopying, recording, scanning, or otherwise without written permission from the publisher. It is illegal to copy this book, post it to a website, or distribute it by any other means without permission.

Ce'Ce Perez asserts the moral right to be identified as the author of this work.

First edition

ISBN: 979-8-9993619-0-5

This book was professionally typeset on Reedsy.

Find out more at reedsy.com

Dedication

Thank you, God, for your guidance,

wisdom, and protection.

Without you, I would not be the woman I am today.

Epigraph

"Every scar tells the story of a heart that chose to keep going."
— Maxine Darrell Thomas

Table of Contents

Dedication _____ *3*

Epigraph _____ *4*

Acknowledgments _____ *8*

Introduction _____ *12*

Letter To The Reader _____ *14*

Lesson 1 _____ *17*

I Didn't Know What I Was Signing Up For _____ *17*

Lesson 2 _____ *23*

Can I Trust Him – Or Just Hope He Won't Hurt Me? *23*

Lesson 3 _____ *29*

When The Fairytale Dies, But We Stay Anyway __ *29*

Lesson 4 _____ *36*

Love Shouldn't Hurt — But Sometimes It Does __ *36*

Lesson 5 _____ *42*

What If Letting Go Is The Key To Getting More? *42*

Lesson 6 _____ *46*

The Surrender That Saved Us _____ *46*

Lesson 7 _____ *51*

Why Am I Always The One Pulling Us Forward? __ *51*

Lesson 8 _____ *56*

Tired Doesn't Mean I'm Done _____ *56*

Lesson 9	*61*
Fighting For Peace At Home	*61*
Lesson 10	*66*
How Do We Build One Home From Two Lives?	*66*
Lesson 11	*69*
Who Is This Man I Married?	*69*
Lesson 12	*76*
Married, But Lonely	*76*
Lesson 13	*82*
When To Speak — And When to Stay Silent	*82*
Lesson 14	*89*
Am I Still That Girl?	*89*
Lesson 15	*95*
What Makes Him Feel Safe With Me?	*95*
Lesson 16	*101*
Submission Isn't A Dirty Word	*101*
Lesson 17	*107*
What Happened To The Flame?	*107*
Lesson 18	*112*
Still Here. Still Fighting. Still Us.	*112*
Lesson 19	*117*
When He Shuts Down	*117*

Lesson 20	*123*
The Tone We Set Without A Word	*123*
Lesson 21	*128*
Bringing Baggage To The Table	*128*
Lesson 22	*133*
It's Not About What Just Happened	*133*
Lesson 23	*139*
Being His Safe Place	*139*
Lesson 24	*143*
Touch Me Like You See Me	*143*
Conclusion	*148*
Lesson By Lesson Scripture Summary	*150*
About The Author	*156*

Acknowledgments

This book is more than a collection of pages—it's a journey of healing, hope, and heart. A reflection of God's grace and the people He placed in my life to help carry me through. I'm grateful that God didn't let me arrive here alone.

To **God**, my source—thank You for walking with me through every chapter of life, not just this one. For strengthening me when I wanted to quit and reminding me that my voice, my story, and my healing still mattered.

To my mother, **Charlotte**—thank you for giving me life and loving me through every season. To my bonus mother, **Martha**—your care for me and my family was always felt, never forced. I am who I am today in part because of the love you both gave in your own ways. And to my mother-in-law, **Carmen**—your love for me has been a blessing I am grateful to have.

To my father, **Albert**, you were the first man to love me. Your presence, protection, and steady example of love gave me something solid to stand on. You'll always be my hero.

To my siblings—**Tuledo, Alberta, Albert, Valnita, Alene**, and **Tomika**—my Howard crew. You've been with me from the beginning, always real, always honest. Thank you for your love, laughter, feedback, and your faith in me.

To **Uncle Curry** and **Aunt Aline** —thank you for showing me what a godly, enduring love looks like. Auntie, you've been my role model and my inspiration for what it means to be a wife. The way you live out that role continues to speak to me more deeply than words ever could.

To my **Carlos**—Thank you for walking beside me through life's highest peaks and hardest valleys. Together, we overcame storms that made us stronger, not weaker. We loved, laughed, struggled, bonded, and built a life that shaped me into the godly woman I became.

To my babies, **Zulemie, Aarianne, Donita,** and **Carlos Jr.**—thank you for your love and support. Your lives are part of our legacy. I see pieces of our journey continuing in each of you.

To my daughter-in-law, **Jasmyne** —thank you for being a part of my writing journey. Your listening heart and transparent perspective are always appreciated.

To my son-in-law, **Daniel Sr** — thank you for your love and support, and for being a part of my writing journey. Your willingness to offer your unique perspective and views is always appreciated.

To my nephew, **Willie** — thank you for always being there with an open ear and offering a creative, checks-and-balances view. Your support has helped me to validate my choices in those moments of self-doubt.

To my brother-in-law, **Anthony, and** my cousin, **Ronald** — thank you both for sharing your perspectives as men and husbands and for offering your biblical insight.

To my brother from another mother, **Eric** — thank you for listening and keeping it real, no matter what.

To my grandsons and my next-generation artistic muses, **Daniel, Zayvion,** and **Aalijah**—your willingness to listen and offer your thoughts on my graphics and other writing ideas is valued and appreciated.

To my sister-friends—**Melba, LaTanya, Linda, Maxine, Robin, Penny, Monica, Tiena, Patricia,** and **Brenda**—thank you for being my support system, my safe space, and my sisters in spirit. You held me up more than you know.

To the women who courageously shared their stories—**Sonya, Janice, Krista, Donna, Michelle, Barbara, Claudia, Aarianne, Linda, Lockquetta, Bonita, Rayshell,** and **Ursula**—thank you for your honesty and for placing your trust in us. Your voices gave this book its soul.

To my writing partner, **Jamela**— *"iron sharpens iron,"* sister—thank you for growing with me and praying with me. You are my A team. What God has instilled in us is now coming to fruition. Get ready!

And finally, to **John**—thank you for being that steady voice of wisdom and grace. You're my constant, my peace, my friend, my confidant. Thank you for your continued encouragement, support, and love; they are appreciated more than you will ever know. You knew that doing this was something I had avoided for a long time, but you encouraged me to be obedient to God's call on my life, and you loved me through the process. I'll forever treasure you for that.

There are so many more I'd love to thank by name, but for now, I pray you know you are all forever in my heart and prayers—thank you. If you've touched my life in any way, know that a part of your lives is in these pages.

With all my love,

Ce'ce Perez

Introduction

I didn't plan to write a book. I didn't even know I was being prepared to.

God started me on this journey long before I had the words, long before I could see the whole picture.

It began in whispered conversations with girlfriends after church, in late-night calls with sisters in tears, in the quiet moments after arguments where I asked God, *"Is this what marriage is supposed to feel like?"*

Then came the moments that humbled me—when I was the one asking for prayer, trying to hold it together, struggling to be the wife I promised I'd be. I didn't know then that every lesson, every piece of wisdom passed down by my aunties and other women who'd walked this road before me, was a seed. I didn't realize I was being prepared not only to receive truth, but also to give it.

This isn't just a book for broken women. It's not just for wives in crisis. It's for every woman who has ever loved a man and tried to figure out how to trust God in the process.

But it's also for the brothers who've asked, "What are women really thinking?" or "What is this list women keep that hard-working brothers like us rarely make?"

Over the years, I've had genuine, raw conversations with men—husbands, brothers, and friends—who genuinely wanted to understand, do better, and love deeper. They didn't need judgment. They needed the truth. And they liked it from someone who wasn't afraid to tell it like it is.

I'm not a licensed counselor. I'm not a therapist. I'm a woman who's lived it. Who's prayed through it; who's cried in it and learned from it. A wife who was fortunate enough to be poured into by women who didn't sugarcoat their stories. They taught me how to fight for my marriage, how to submit without shrinking, how to speak truth without shame, and how to stay soft when life hardened around me.

This book is the overflow of that journey.

It's not perfect. It's not polished.

But it's honest. And I pray its healing.

Ready? Let's go!

Letter To The Reader

Hey Sis,

I'm glad you picked this up. Whether someone who loves you handed you a copy or you found it while searching for something relatable and authentic—either way, I don't believe it was by accident you're reading this.

Please note My experiences may not mirror yours. There isn't a cookie cutter formula to fix each and every one of our challenges. I'm a wife whose experienced life and walked through seasons that cracked my heart in places I never knew existed. I've been the one silently struggling while offering my shoulder to a sister who was barely hanging on and was blessed to learn from some wise women as they modeled their routine, showering love on their husbands with a strength that didn't need to be loud to be powerful.

This book offers 24 lessons for the women who are somewhere between "we made it" and "we almost didn't." It's for the tired woman, yes. But it's also for the steady one. The one who's healed. The one who is still waiting for their healing. And for the one who's looking for words to share with a friend in the thick of it.

No matter where you're in your marriage—whether you're beginning, rebuilding, or barely holding on—I pray these lessons feel like you're sitting across from a sister who sees you. Who won't sugarcoat it? Who knows that being a godly wife doesn't mean being perfect but being honest, humble, and faithful.

I'm not here to force anything on you—not my faith, not my story, and not my perspective. I know that **my relationship with God has saved my sanity,** well-being, and marriage on more occasions than I can count.

It gave me peace when I had none, helped me stay when I was ready to bounce, and showed me how to leave behind what was limiting my growth. Religion didn't change me. It was a relationship—with God and with women who walked beside me.

Take what speaks to you. Sit with it. Share it. Wrestle with it. And when you're ready, pass it on. Because somebody out there needs what you just received. Somebody's waiting for a reminder that they're not crazy, not weak, not alone.

We don't heal in silence. We heal in sisterhood.

With grace, grit, and all my love,

Ce'ce

Lesson 1

I Didn't Know What I Was Signing Up For

Red, black, and white.

These were the colors I had dreamed of for my wedding long before I knew what marriage truly was or what it would require.

Don't act like I was the only one with these childhood dreams.

Many of us grew up with dreams of our ideal wedding.

From the days of baby dolls and fairy tales, we'd fantasize about the details of our wedding, from the perfect color pairing to the time of year, from our dress design to where we'd marry, be it an immaculate church, a candlelit park, or on the sands of a coastal beach.

The only missing piece that would complete our dream, the most critical piece, is who would be our lucky groom.

One day, our king will come; he will love us unconditionally, and our lives will be better than we'd imagined. Delusional much? Possibly. Can marital bliss be achieved? Absolutely! However, it requires us and our husbands to work together.

When our relationships were new, we'd make goo-goo eyes at one another, dress alike, or wear the same color. We'd share messages that only the two of us understood. We'd tell ourselves that everything we were doing was to create memories we'd one day share with our future kids.

- Dating – Check
- Engagement – Check
- Proposal – Check
- Wedding – Check

So…now what?

Does life slide into our DMs to take up permanent residence?

Are we both given some invisible boxes with details on what I needed to be his wife and something also for him on how to be my husband?

Is love measured by the number of good days we share? What would we do when good days are few and far between? Like some distant memory? Or…is it more to this story?

Love Was Built on Purpose

"It is not good that man should be alone; I will make him a helper comparable to him." —Genesis 2:18 (NKJV)

Reading this scripture is a reminder to me that God has specifically created someone for me.

He, God, wasn't talking about the kind of love we read about in romance novels or seen in movies.

God was talking about His purpose for us.

Marriage isn't something we just check off our bucket list; it is a companionship and a journey that two people, husband and wife, choose to embark on together.

The journey has its own challenges—peaks and valleys that sway one way or another, warm and cool seasons—that require alignment and trust from both of us, wives in our husbands. Every aspect of our journey will strengthen our foundation as we grow and build together.

To be clear, we were not created to fix our husbands, nor were our husbands created to fix us. God has already taken that job.

Where It Goes Left

So, how did we get here? When did we start believing that love would be easy, automatic, and magical—every day?

Whose Kool-Aid did we foolishly drink?

We were so fixated on the fantasy that we were unable to see the truth.

TV love — is not covenant love.

Culture has conditioned us to believe:

Real love doesn't hurt.

If we tell ourselves he's "the one," he will keep us happy and never disappoint us.

What's meant to be, it's that simple.

Lies lies, ALL lies — It's unrealistic, made up, and pure fantasy.

Real love shows up when we don't feel like it and stays when everything in us wants to leave.

Running on Empty

Many of us believe that once we're married, our spouses will fill the emptiness, void, and space created by years of brokenness, past and present.

This logic has a huge problem. It's not possible. No human is capable of fulfilling this for any of us.

"We love because He first loved us" —1 John 4:19 (KJV)

I've always found comfort in knowing God loves me, even when I didn't feel I deserved it.

If we close our hearts to God and don't allow Him to heal us, our spouses may feel like they're failing us. How fair is that to them, our husbands, or our marriages?

- We can't possibly expect anyone to fix what they didn't break.
- We must be willing to let God in and allow Him to guide us during those tough days, even when we don't feel like we can give love but feel tempted to make demands or insults.

What Happens After the Vows

- We realize love alone doesn't pay bills.
- We see habits we've overlooked, or thought were "cute," but now, they pose problems.

- We find out conflict isn't what breaks us — silence does.
- We learn that *"unconditional love"* doesn't mean *"unlimited foolishness."*

Marriage doesn't necessarily heal loneliness; sometimes, it can even magnify it. That's why we must remain connected to God, not just to one another.

Solutions for the Messy Middle:

- **Have Real Conversations**: Surface-level conversations are surface-level, with no real connections. Go deeper.
- **Guard the Purpose**: When we're mad, we should ask ourselves: *"Is this about pride or purpose?"*
- **Forgive Fast and Often:** Forgiveness isn't a gift to our husbands; it's a gift to ourselves.
- **Grow Together**: Stop expecting a finished product. We're both a work in progress.
- **Pray Even When It's Awkward**: Some fights only God can fix.

Contract vs. Covenant

The world teaches, *"I'll stay as long as he makes me happy."*

God teaches, *"I'll stay because I made a promise."*

His love endures forever.

> **"Give thanks to the God of heaven. His love endures forever." —Psalm 136:26 (NIV)**

Covenant love mirrors that. It's not about convenience; it's about commitment.

Love Is a Choice

1 Corinthians 13 is a reminder that love is patient, kind, not easily angered, and keeps no record of wrongs.

This isn't a casual kind of love. It's invested work.

- Choosing to love on easy days? That's cute.
- Choosing to love when we feel misunderstood, unseen, or frustrated? That's a covenant.

Reflection Questions:

1. What unrealistic ideas about love and marriage did you carry into your vows—and where did they come from?
2. Was it something you saw in movies, believed as a child, or learned from others?
3. In what ways have you looked to your spouse to heal a part of you that only God can reach?
4. What intentional actions can you take this week to nurture your marriage as a covenant, not a contract?

Lesson 2

Can I Trust Him – Or Just Hope He Won't Hurt Me?

I recall the moment I first realized I wasn't entirely trusting him. I'd sent my husband to the store to pick up some personal items for me, you know, female items. When he returned, he'd gotten the wrong thing.

He'd grabbed a box of Depends instead of the sanitary napkins I'd originally sent him for. Ugh! Mind you, this wasn't a life-or-death situation, and although, at the time, I laughed it off, my attempt to lighten the moment eased his need for my approval, but in the back of my mind I told myself he couldn't follow directions. Little things like this, especially early in a marriage, can lead to sharp words and hurt feelings. We were still finding our way and learning how to lean into one another.

For him, he thought he was doing something nice for me. He'd worked hard all day and stopped by the store, asking me if I needed anything. When I saw the Depends, I felt insulted instead of seeing it for what it was, a simple mistake.

Looking back, I know that it wasn't about the pads. It was about the fear I hadn't named yet. My lesson from this instance was to be specific in my request and to not make something bigger than it was. If your husband is like mine, they expect us to find something wrong in what they do. Sis, it's not that serious. Chill. Enjoy your man.

At that moment, I wasn't reacting to him—I was responding to every man in my past who had let me down. I mentally felt as if I was holding my breath, waiting for the other shoe to drop, for him to eventually say, "I'm done," but… it never came.

I struggled with knowing how to rest in love for a long time because before then, love had never felt like a safe place. It always came with terms, disappointments, or, eventually, an expiration date.

That's when I knew it wasn't just about trusting my husband. It was about trusting God. Trusting that He would hold me even if things didn't go the way I hoped.

We can't love deeply if we're always expecting him to drop us.

How many of us have ever felt so anxious or nervous that we might do or say something that, at any minute, he won't want us anymore?

These fears are what we carry into our marriages, like worn luggage where the zipper is now held together by pieces of thread. We've told ourselves that when people say they are with us forever, what they really mean is that they are with us until we do something they don't like or say something that cancels us out.

With all of our good intentions, these scars make us hesitant to believe we can find and keep true love. So…with that, we love with one foot in and the other halfway out the door.

Is this love? No. Its fear prancing around in a pretty little dress.

And fear will always rob you of the real thing.

Why Trusting God Changes the Game

When we anchor our hearts in God, we're no longer asking someone else to be our lifeline.

We stop depending on him to be perfect or to make us feel safe. We stop putting pressure on every moment, wanting to prove something to him instead of believing in ourselves. We stop falling apart every time life doesn't follow the script we've written in our heads.

"Trust in the LORD with all your heart And lean not on your own understanding; In all your ways acknowledge Him, And He shall direct your paths." — Proverbs 3:5-6 (NKJV)

When God is our anchor, we will love loosely — not recklessly, but free. We can love because we're content and not desperate.

Trust Teaches You to Hold, Not Strangle

Absolute trust doesn't mean we'll never get hurt again.

It means hurt won't destroy us. It will still sting or even knock the wind out of us, just as it did before. The difference this time is that we're gaining wisdom and strength. Our legs may buckle, but we have a foundation we can lean on…God. He's got us.

A woman who trusts God can stand tall in the middle of a betrayal and say, *"You may hurt me, but this doesn't define me. My God has already done that."*

Even when, at times, these words are uttered or thought of, but for some reason, they don't feel true in our hearts, don't give up. Continue to say them, believe them, and trust in God.

Each day, if we keep our heads lifted and our focus on Him, our storms will pass. We will become stronger and wiser than we ever thought possible.

We won't chase love. We won't play mind games. We won't crumble under pressure.

We will love with open hearts and arms.

Why? Because we know what God has for us cannot be stolen, sabotaged, or scared away.

Trusting Without a Map

Faith doesn't mean we will know everything or have all of the answers. We won't know which steps to take on our journey.

Sometimes, faith looks like walking through some dark places with nothing but God's soft whisper urging us forward. Keep going.

Sometimes faith:

- looks like we need to stand still and stay put when we feel misunderstood.
- looks like praying when we're so angry that praying is the last thing we want to do.
- looks like loving even when we feel like we're not loved in return.

"Blessed is she who has believed that the Lord would fulfill his promises to her." — Luke 1:45 (NIV)

Trust is messy, painful, and costly.

But trust this, it's the only soil where real love can truly grow.

Learning Love from the Only One Who Gets It Right

God doesn't love us because we earned it.

He loves us when we're stubborn. He loves us when we're at our worst. He loves us when we don't understand and even when we get it wrong, time and again.

Once we get a taste of that kind of love, it will wreck us—in the best way.

We will:

- stop trying to control everything.
- stop demanding guarantees.
- start covering our homes, our husbands, and even our own fragile hearts with the kind of grace we've received.

Love becomes less about managing outcomes and more about magnifying God.

When God Is Our Center, We're Unshakable

We're no longer being tossed around by bad days, crushed by unmet expectations, or living in a reactive mode.

We're steady because our hearts have been claimed by God, who doesn't change.

That steadiness spills over into every argument, every disappointment, and every *"I don't know how we're going to fix this"* moment.

"You will keep in perfect peace those whose minds are steadfast, because they trust in you." — Isaiah 26:3 (NIV)

Reflection Questions:

1. Are you building your love on God's unshakable truth or shaky emotions?
2. Where have you been loving with fear instead of faith?
3. What would trusting God with your whole heart change about how you love today?

Lesson 3

When The Fairytale Dies, But We Stay Anyway

Can I let you in on a secret? As a little girl, I loved Cinderella, Snow White, and the Wizard of Oz. The idea of an attractive prince showing up at just the right time to rescue the distressed damsel fascinated me.

It wasn't until I was an adult that I realized these women were all in difficult situations. Before the fairy tale lovers shoot daggers at me with their side eyes, let me explain. Each of these women was living a mundane life they wished to escape.

Cinderella was a tortured servant to her stepmother and sisters. Snow White ran away to escape her wicked witch stepmother, who wanted her dead. And poor Dorothy, when her family made her feel like a worrisome child, she longed for a different life far, far away. Sound familiar?

Some of us watched these shows so much as children that the heroine's plight became our plight, their situation became our situations, their wants, and so on.

Did I miss anything?

Picture this—a man rides in on a horse and connects with a troubled young girl who is facing situational challenges. Promises of love were meant to heal every wound and an expectation that escaping to a different life would make everything better and make sense. Simple. Wrong.

We bought into the fairy tale.

The fantasy seemed believable, but it wasn't real love. It never was.

There's no soundtrack playing in the background, no crowd gathered silently cheering us on as we're swept away by our dashing prince, and no magical ending tied neatly together with a beautiful bow.

Real Love Doesn't Come to Save Us

Let's be really honest: godly, faithful, and good-hearted men aren't meant to come to our rescue. In fact, they have no idea that we're expecting them to do so.

They were never supposed to.

If we really think about it, Jesus has already taken that job.

The Danger of Waiting to Be Rescued

For some of us, we think that marriage will fix what hurts is a fallacy, a fabrication, a setup.

- Husbands aren't here to erase our insecurities.
- Love can't erase our fears.
- Affection can't heal our traumas.

When we put weight like this on the men we love, we're not getting security— we're getting constant disappointment.

We may resent them for not saving us from things they weren't created to fix.

Only God Can Heal What's Broken

"I, even I, am the Lord, and apart from me there is no savior." — Isaiah 43:11 (NIV)

There's only one Savior, Healer, Redeemer.

It's not our husbands.

Our husbands can:

- Lead us,
- Provide for us,
- Love us,
- Support us and
- Walk beside us

Our husbands can't:

- Erase our pain
- Make us whole
- Heal us
- Save us
- Or redeem us

Only God can do that.

The Problem with Pedestals

Sometimes, we don't realize it has happened. We'll meet a guy, things feel good, then suddenly he's placed on some superficial pedestal, a place he never asked for. The men become God-like in our eyes, or at least we elevate them to that level.

We give them invisible crowns, deeming them our "rescuer," "healer," or even our "king of happiness" — that is until something happens when the guy doesn't meet our expectations. Something inside of us cracks, and our idea of them changes.

We feel crushed and disillusioned. Suddenly, we realize that these men are human, not who we had made them out to be.

When we idolize men, whether out of fear of being alone, past hurts, or the belief that we can fix it this time, every flaw will feel like a betrayal. Mistakes feel like abandonment, and arguments feel like threats.

Fear of losing grips us so tightly that we are willing to do almost anything to keep him with us and happy.

Because if this man was supposed to save us, why are we still hurting?

Answer: because that expectation was never for this man to carry.

God Is Not Sending a Prince. He's Sending a Partner.

God's plan isn't about being rescued. It's about being ready.

- Ready to love, not cling.
- Ready to partner, not demand.
- Ready to build, not beg.

"My help comes from the Lord, who made heaven and earth." — Psalm 121:2 (ESV)

Our foundation was ALWAYS supposed to be God, never a man.

When we live our lives anchored in God, we don't leave marriage empty, waiting for our husbands to fill us. We come complete — ready to pour, receive, partner, and build something lasting.

What a Good Man Can and Can't Do

A Godly man can cover his wife in prayer. He can encourage our dreams. He can be a safe place.

But he is not our source.

He's not supposed to be the well we drink from. He's supposed to build on the foundation of God that's already laid for us.

"Therefore, everyone who hears these words of mine and puts them into practice is like a wise man who built his house on the rock… it did not fall, because it had its foundation on the rock." — Matthew 7:24-25 (NIV)

This marriage can weather storms — not because it's perfect, but because it's anchored and built on a solid foundation.

Stop Waiting to Be Chosen

What is the biggest lie that rescue fantasies sell?

- That our story doesn't start until someone "picks" us.
- That love validates us. That marriage completes us.

These are all LIES

We've already been chosen.

"But ye are a chosen generation, a royal priesthood, a holy nation, His own special people, that you may proclaim the praises of Him who is called you out of darkness into His marvelous light. "— 1 Peter 2:9 (NKJV)

God called us worthy before any man ever knew our names.

- We're not waiting to be loved to start living.
- We're already walking on purpose.
- We're already full.
- We're already loved.

Truth Versus Fantasy

We need to step away from the fairy tales and step into reality.

- Relationships are built on faith, not fantasy.
- Partners who stand with us and not over us.
- Love anchored in God and created on fragile dreams.

No glass slipper. No magical rescue. No perfect man.

Just two imperfect people, rooted in a perfect God, building something real.

Reflection Questions:

1. What are you still waiting for someone to fix, fill, or affirm?

2. Have you placed expectations on him to complete or validate you?
3. What would it look like to live today as someone already chosen, whole, and loved?
4. How would your love shift if you lived from a place of fullness rather than need?

Lesson 4

Love Shouldn't Hurt — But Sometimes It Does

When love costs more than we expected—but gives back more than we imagined

We rarely talk about what it feels like to still love someone who's hurt us—not with their fists, but with their forgetfulness, silence, withdrawal, and inconsistency. This kind of pain doesn't necessarily leave physical bruises, but mental bruises, scars that are just as bad if not worse. They damage our hopes and beliefs in our partner. And most importantly…they sometimes leave a lasting impact.

At one time, I believed love was supposed to be a quick fix for most broken things, a healing, a means to make life feel and look brighter. Although this version was the one many of us were taught, or at least led to believe in.

Thinking about those childhood fairy tales that never said love would be hard, but this… this is confusing. Church said love was a blessing, but what they didn't say was what to do when the blessing left us feeling broken. The world tells us to love ourselves first and walk away when it's bad, but that advice doesn't work when we've made a covenant and still hope that what we've done is redeemable.

No one prepares us to love through our disillusions.

No one tells us that loving someone so deeply can sometimes hurt just as deeply.

But can we talk about it—for real?

When Loving Leaves, We're Wounded

Many nights I'd lie in bed with my husband beside me, and yet I felt alone. It wasn't because something was wrong. It was because I just felt this distance between us… Literally. Other times, there were moments when I wondered, "Is it supposed to feel this empty?" Don't get me wrong. I loved him, and he loved me—but love just didn't feel like it was enough.

I wasn't angry with him. I just felt…tired. I was tired of feeling like everything was mine to carry. Tired of feeling like I had to be the glue that held us, our family, our life, together. Tired of praying and not seeing instant results. Tired of hoping for a version of us that I wasn't sure existed, at least not anymore.

And yet, I told myself, "You know you're not going anywhere." So, what did I do? I stayed. Why? Because I believed that God didn't bring us together for me to give up when we were in the valley. I thought that God could still breathe on what looked dry. That something holy could still live in what felt hard. And that I, like many of us, had to unlearn some toxic beliefs to get there.

The Myth That Real Love Doesn't Hurt

We've romanticized love to the point that anything challenging feels like a red flag. But sometimes, the flag isn't…red—it's **real**. And real love will cost us. It will ask us to die to our egos. To choose forgiveness when the world tells us to protect ourselves. To speak when we want to shut down. To stay vulnerable and transparent even after we've been disappointed.

Love isn't soft all the time. Sometimes, love is steel wrapped in skin. Other times, it's bleeding and believing at the same time.

Real love **hurts** because it's genuine and something we, as humans, feel. But that hurt doesn't mean it's broken beyond repair. Sometimes, it means God is pulling something deeper out of us both.

God Doesn't Waste pain

Psalm 34:18 says, *"The Lord is close to the brokenhearted."*

This isn't a metaphor—it's a promise.

God saw our tears in the bathroom. He heard our prayers at 3am. He was with us in the moments we felt dismissed and even when we started to doubt if our love mattered.

God wasn't ignoring us then, nor is He ignoring us now. He's shaping us.

This doesn't mean He caused the hurt. But it does mean He's not letting it go unused. Every tear sown in faith is a seed for restoration. He's not done writing our story.

When Loving Hurts, It Reveals

Sometimes, pain reveals what remains unhealed within us.

Some of us may believe that what hurt the most wasn't just what our husbands did or didn't do—it was the narratives we attached to those moments.

"He forgot again" became *"I'm not important enough to matter."*

"He's quiet tonight" became *"He doesn't want me."*

"He didn't notice I was upset" became *"My needs don't matter."*

The enemy loves to twist wounds into identity. But God speaks something better: *"You are seen. You are valued. You are chosen—even when he doesn't show it the way you need."*

The pain becomes a mirror. Not to condemn but to invite us into a more profound healing.

Grace Doesn't Excuse—It Empowers

Let me be clear: grace doesn't mean accepting emotional abuse or staying in something unsafe. Boundaries are biblical. Wisdom is godly.

But if our marriage is struggling—not toxic—and we're trying to love through seasons of distance, grace can hold the gap.

Grace is powerful. It doesn't erase truth—it invites redemption. It gives room for change. And sometimes, grace is what keeps a door cracked long enough for growth to walk in.

We're Not Alone in This

When we're hurting in love, know this:

- We're not weak for feeling weary.
- We're not failing because things aren't perfect.
- We're not forgotten by the God who sees us, even when our husbands don't seem to.

Our story isn't over yet. This might be the middle—the part where character is built, where God redefines our view of love, and where we learn to fight not against each other but *for* each other.

Love That Survives the Pain Grows Deeper

I won't lie and pretend it was easy because it wasn't. However, I can say that part of the problem was my own perspective on what I thought I was versus what God was bringing me into. I've seen God breathe in broken places. I've seen dry bones dance. In awe, I've witnessed God work things out through me, bringing us back from moments I thought would have ended us.

But…we stayed.

Because we stopped trying to fix each other and started letting God fix what was underneath.

Because I learned that loving hard didn't mean loving blindly.

It meant loving **bravely**.

Reflection Questions

1. Where have you confused pain in love with failure in love?
2. What narratives are you attaching to your partner's actions that may not be rooted in truth?
3. How can you invite God into the healing instead of trying to carry it all alone?
4. Are there boundaries you need to clarify—not to punish, but to protect?
5. What would grace look like for both of you in this season?
6. How can you move from hurt to healing without losing your softness?

Lesson 5

What If Letting Go Is The Key To Getting More?

Love is powerful. But when love turns into performance—when our "yes" to him becomes a "no" to ourselves—it stops being love and starts being a form of survival. I've lived this. Many of us have.

We bend, shape, and shrink just to keep the peace, to protect his ego, and to maintain the marriage. But a love that requires us to disappear isn't love—it's imbalance.

We enter marriage ready to become "one," but if we're not careful, we'll become none. Our voices will fade under compromise. Our dreams will wither in the shadow of "support." And the version of us that God so beautifully crafted will quietly die behind a smile.

The Silent Surrender

We give and give. At first, it's small—letting our husbands lead, letting him decide, letting him win. But over time, if it's not mutual, we begin to vanish and resent him for the things we allowed to happen.

And here's the thing: many of us watched our mothers, aunties, or grandmothers do the same. We saw them fade into the background. Faithful, yes. Present, always. But full of resentment, regret, and what-ifs they never said out loud.

So, we enter marriage guarded. Or we overcompensate. And neither works.

God didn't ask us to lose ourselves to love Him. He asked us to be whole with Him. The moment we begin hiding who we are to keep the marriage, the foundation has already started to crack.

"Whoever finds their life will lose it, and whoever loses their life for my sake will find it." —Matthew 10:39 (NIV)

This scripture doesn't mean we should lose ourselves to our husbands. It means we should surrender ourselves to God—and in doing so, we find a life rooted in truth, not fear.

Boundaries Aren't Barriers

There's a difference between selflessness and self-abandonment. Marriage will always require compromise—but it should never cost us our identity.

Set the boundary. Protect our voice. Communicate our needs, not from a place of defense but from a place of value. We were made for more than silent suffering. We were made to partner. To grow. To thrive.

When many of us draw those lines, we don't push him away—we invite him into a relationship with the real us.

Healing the Fear of Letting Go

Let's be honest. A lot of us hold on tight because we're scared. Scared to trust. Scared to need. Scared to let go and be disappointed again.

But holding on too tightly—controlling, micromanaging, over-functioning—will drain us and disconnect us from our husbands. Real intimacy requires space. Real love involves trust.

I had to learn this the hard way. My healing didn't come when I tried to change him. It came when I surrendered my fears to God. When I stopped trying to control everything in our lives, I stopped trying to make sure:

- we would be okay no matter what
- everything was covered

Instead, I asked, *"Lord, who did You make me to be in this marriage?"*

That's when I found peace. That's when I remembered that the best gift, I could give my husband was the version of me that God designed—not the version I had morphed into, the "superwoman" who thought she could do it all.

God's Love Doesn't Cancel Yours

We don't have to choose between being a good wife and being our authentic selves. We can be both. We can serve and be strong. Submit and still speak. Love and have limits.

God's design for marriage was never about one partner disappearing for the other to shine. It's about mutual submission. It's about two becoming one without either one being erased.

"So, they are no longer two, but one flesh. Therefore, what God has joined together, let no one separate." —Matthew 19:6 (NIV)

No one includes us. We don't have to separate ourselves from ourselves to stay married. We don't have to dim our light in the name of unity.

God joined us together with our husbands as we are, not as the watered-down version of us because we were afraid of being ourselves. Girl… let's not do that.

Let go of the fear. Let go of the need to please. Let go of the belief that our voice is too much, or our dreams are too big. Release it all—to receive everything God really has for us.

Reflection Questions:

1. What parts of yourself have you silenced or sacrificed out of fear?
2. Where has over-functioning become a way of proving your worth?
3. What would it look like to show up as your whole self—loved by God, seen by your husband, and led by peace?

Lesson 6

The Surrender That Saved Us

Before we can submit, we have to surrender the wound behind the wall—the fear that if we yield, we'll disappear.

Let's be honest—submission is one of those words that triggers reactions. For some of us, it sounds like silence. For others, control. And for too many, it feels like a threat to everything we've worked hard to build—our voices, our independence, our strength.

But when God speaks of submission in marriage, He's not talking about erasure. He's talking about alignment. About partnership. About love that honors order without compromising identity.

"Wives, submit yourselves to your own husbands as you do to the Lord." —Ephesians 5:22 (NIV)

This verse has been twisted, weaponized, and thrown like a grenade into conversations that needed healing, not harm. But if we read on—

"Husbands, love your wives, just as Christ loved the church and gave himself up for her."—we realize this isn't about dominance. It's about mutual surrender. It's about covenant.

When Submission Feels Like Swallowing Your Voice

It doesn't always feel good. Especially when we're married to men who are still learning how to lead. Or when we're carrying wounds from past relationships or even childhood trauma. Submission, to some of us, feels like disappearing. But it's not.

Submission isn't silence. It's a strength that bows to God's order, not man's ego. It says, "I trust God enough to guide him—even when I don't see it yet." And that's not a weakness. That's power wrapped in wisdom.

Grace Isn't Passive—It's a Strategy

Grace doesn't mean letting things slide. It means knowing when to speak and how to articulate your thoughts effectively. When our husbands miss it, grace says, "I'll love you enough to cover you while God corrects you." That doesn't mean being quiet when we need to speak up. It means choosing our words with maturity, not out of rage.

"She speaks with wisdom, and faithful instruction is on her tongue." —Proverbs 31:26 (NIV)

Real submission is bold. It doesn't curl up in the corner. It kneels in prayer before it moves in love. It's saying, *"God, make me wise enough to love him even when it's hard."*

Submission is NOT…

- Staying silent in abuse.
- Accepting disrespect.
- A pass for dysfunction.

God never called us to be doormats.

But He did call us to live by His principles. And submission, when done under God's direction, becomes a posture of trust, not oppression.

It's a spiritual alignment that says, "Even if he's learning, even if I'm frustrated, I'm not letting my pride wreck our peace."

Forgiveness and Surrender Go Hand-in-Hand

We can't truly submit if our hearts are full of grudges. We'll hold back love while keeping score of his wrongdoings.

Sometimes, the only thing blocking our breakthrough is the bitterness we refuse to let go of.

Letting go of past offenses doesn't make us naive—it makes us free.

And here's the truth: submission without forgiveness is fake. Because our bodies can surrender while our hearts are still in rebellion.

God is calling us to a clean heart, not just one that is compliant.

We Can Be Strong and Still Submit

One of the biggest lies culture tells us is that submission makes us weak. But sis, listen—there's nothing more substantial than a woman who can yield when every part of her wants to fight.

We know our value. We can speak our truths. But we also know when to hold back and pray instead of pounce.

- That's not playing small. That's playing smart.
- That's love with layers. And that's the kind of strength God honors.

When He's Still Learning to Lead

It's tough when the man we married isn't quite the spiritual leader we hoped for.

We want him to pray first. We want him to cover us. But he's still growing. And sometimes, that gap frustrates us more than we're willing to admit.

This is where submission gets real.

It means trusting God's process in our husband, not trying to rush it or take over.

Pray for him. Speak life over him. And remember—God doesn't need our help fixing him. He needs our faith.

Submission Is a Love Language

It's not the kind that fits in a meme. But the type that shows up when nobody's watching.

When we respect him even after an argument. When we cover his flaws instead of posting our frustrations. When we choose unity over being right.

That's what love with roots looks like.

Submission is one of the ways we say: "I believe in us. I believe in you. And most of all, I believe in the God who brought us together."

Reflection Questions:

1. What fears or past wounds make submission difficult for you?
2. Where are you resisting alignment—not just with your husband, but with God?
3. What would it look like to submit with wisdom, not weakness, this week?

Lesson 7

Why Am I Always The One Pulling Us Forward?

There's something I wish someone had told me earlier: just because we're married doesn't mean we'll always walk in spiritual sync. And that's not necessarily failure—it might just be the process.

I grew up hearing scriptural-based warnings from pastors in the pulpit, receiving words of wisdom from church mothers, as well as unsolicited advice from the women in our neighborhood, and most often from my mom, aunts, and their group of mother hens.

They instilled in me this notion that something was wrong if my husband and I weren't praying together every morning. If we weren't fasting at the same time or reading the Word side by side, something was definitely broken.

But what I eventually learned was this—spiritual alignment isn't always identical in motion. Sometimes, it's shared direction—even when the pace is different.

In all honesty, there were times early on when I felt as if I was the only one chasing after God. I'd joined a church, served in the choir, and read scriptures to him while we lay in bed. I prayed over him, all while he snored, anointed his head and heart with oil.

I watched and waited for him to have his Aha moment, the one when he would step into what I believed was God's purpose for his life. It hurt when I couldn't see any inkling of him getting it. And it made me wonder: "God, did I miss it? Am I the only one who is supposed to carry this thing in this season?"

Deep inside, I knew I wasn't alone.

What It Really Means to Be "*Yoked*"

We hear this scripture all the time: "***Do not be unequally yoked…***" —2 Corinthians 6:14 (AMP). But what does that look like inside a marriage when our husband isn't completely disconnected from God—just not walking with HIM the way we are.

See, the yoke was a wooden bar that connected two oxen and was used to keep them working in the same field. But if one moved faster than the other—or dragged the other along—neither of them could walk straight. The field suffered. The mission stalled. And both grew tired.

That's what it felt like in my home. I wasn't angry at him—I was tired. Tired of praying alone. Tired of feeling unseen. Tired of waiting on him to "catch up" while I silently blamed myself for marrying out of alignment. But one day, God stopped me in my tracks and said, "You're not dragging him. You're also not walking alone. You're walking with Me."

It's His Journey, Too

Sometimes, we mistake spiritual leadership for spiritual speed. We want our husbands to "lead us" but forget that leadership isn't always loud. It isn't always expressive. And it's definitely not about who posts more devotionals.

The truth? He may be seeking God in a way that differs from ours. And that's okay.

Marriage isn't about one of us being the spiritual parent. It's about building a home where growth is possible. That includes grace for each other's pace.

I used to take his silence for apathy. I told myself that his lack of spiritual language meant a lack of depth. But God showed me—he was growing. Quietly. Inwardly. At his own rhythm. And I had to stop interrupting his process just because it didn't mirror mine.

Let Our Life Be the Sermon

When I finally let go of "*spiritual control*," I started seeing fruit. Not because I pushed. But because I paused.

I stopped lecturing. Stopped guilting my husband into Bible studies. Stopped looking disappointed when he didn't do things my way. I let God have that space—and focused on what I could do.

I modeled peace. I walked in joy. I served with integrity. I prayed—not just for him, but over him. And when he started asking questions or reflecting out loud, I didn't pounce on the opportunity to preach. I listened and gave him space. And slowly, our spiritual life began to shift—not through force, but through faith.

Love Draws—It Doesn't Drag

I don't know where many of our marriages are today. Some of us may be in a season where we're carrying all the spiritual weight.

Some of us may be exhausted from feeling like it's all on us. But hear me:

- We are not his savior.
- We are not the Holy Spirit.
- We are our husband's wives.

We're called to love, not fix. To encourage, not convict. To build, not shame.

Even when we feel like we're doing all the spiritual heavy lifting, God sees it. And He honors it. The seeds we're planting now, with tears, will one day bloom with fruit we never expected.

Let our walk be steady. Let our prayers be gentle. Let's live lives that shift our husbands' hearts.

Building Not Intimidating

So, here's the key: don't give up. Don't give in to bitterness or resentment. Don't assume just because our husbands aren't where we are, they'll never get there. Our consistency is working. Our love is planting seeds. Our gentleness is preaching louder than any sermon ever could.

And maybe, just maybe, like the story of so many women of faith whose husbands found God through the quiet strength of their wives—we'll look back and see that we weren't dragging him after all. We were paving the path home.

"The wise woman builds her house, but with her own hands the foolish one tears hers down."—Proverbs 14:1 (NIV)

"Let us not become weary in doing good, for at the proper time we will reap a harvest if we do not give up."— Galatians 6:9 (NIV)

Reflection Questions:

1. Are you creating an environment that invites spiritual growth or demands spiritual performance?
2. What would it look like to release your husband to grow at his own pace?
3. Where can you grow in consistency and grace in your own walk?

Lesson 8

Tired Doesn't Mean I'm Done

Many wives are too embarrassed to admit this, but sometimes…we get tired.

Not just physically tired—though that's true, too. I'm talking about soul-tired.

Emotionally exhausted. Drained from giving, serving, praying, forgiving, covering, explaining, hoping, and trying… while wondering if our effort is even being seen. Much less appreciated.

Marriage is beautiful, but it can also be a lot of work. And sometimes, that work feels incredibly one-sided.

We ask ourselves questions like:

- "Why am I the only one fighting for this?"
- "Does he even notice I'm struggling?"
- "How long can I keep this up before I lose myself completely?"

If that's where some of us are—breathe. We're not broken, and we're not alone.

The Breaking Point

We may have already released our need to control his spiritual walk. And maybe we're no longer feeling like we're dragging our husbands spiritually like we thought we were.

But the weight still lingers. The exhaustion isn't just about spiritual mismatch—it's emotional depletion.

There are moments when the effort feels heavier than the hope. The love we once poured out so freely now comes with hesitation. Our prayers feel repetitive. Our hearts feel ignored.

- We've tried to communicate—he shuts down.
- We've tried to initiate change—but he gets defensive.
- We've brought it to God—yet nothing seems to shift.

We start to wonder, *"Is it supposed to be this hard?"*

"In this world you will have trouble. But take heart! I have overcome the world." —John 16:33 (NIV)

No one told us that sometimes the most challenging part of faithfulness isn't resisting temptation—it's holding onto love when we're running on empty.

Worn Down, Not Worn Out

Feeling tired doesn't mean we're weak; it simply means we're human. But just because we're worn down doesn't mean we're done.

We are allowed to feel what we feel. But we're not meant to live in emotional burnout.

Feelings can cloud faith. Fatigue can distort perspective. What feels like failure may actually be the beginning of deeper endurance.

"Let us not become weary in doing good, for at the proper time we will reap a harvest if we do not give up." — *Galatians 6:9 (NIV)*

A hard season doesn't equal a bad marriage. Every marriage goes through periods where one spouse carries more of the burden. What matters is how we handle those stretches.

Love Without Losing Ourselves

Trying doesn't mean silencing our voices. It doesn't mean abandoning our identity to keep the peace. It means showing up with honesty, integrity, and intention.

- We can love without excusing poor behavior.
- We can serve without being used.
- We can be soft without being silent.

Trying now might look different than it did before.

It might mean letting go of being the fixer. It might mean releasing expectations. It might mean laying down resentment—not because our husband deserves it, but because our peace does.

Trying Looks Different Now

This isn't about adjusting our husband's pace. It's about what to do when we're tired of walking altogether.

Trying might look like:

- Praying more than we speak.
- Fasting instead of fighting.
- Stepping back emotionally so God can step in spiritually.

- Seeking counseling—alone or together.
- Choosing silence instead of sarcasm.
- Worshiping through our weeping.

"Come to me, all you who are weary and burdened, and I will give you rest." —Matthew 11:28 (NIV)

Striving is fear-based: *"If I don't fix this, it will fall apart."*

Trying is faith-based: *"God, I'm tired, but I'm trusting You to sustain what I can't."*

There's a holy kind of effort that doesn't burn us out. It builds us up.

Check Our Source

We weren't meant to hold it all. We were meant to abide.

Many of us try to love when we're emotionally and physically empty. We pour out peace, grace, and patience—but haven't let God refill us.

When was the last time any of us sat in God's presence—not for our marriage, but for our soul?

We should let Him pour back into us. Let Him minister to the wife—not just the warrior.

"But those who wait on the Lord shall renew their strength…" —Isaiah 40:31 (NKJV)

We're Not Crazy for Caring

Some people will tell us to stop trying. To protect our peace. To "do you." But they don't know the prayers we've prayed, the promises we have received, or the assignment God gave us for our marriage.

Yes—there are times when it's best to walk away. However, there are also times to rest, reset, and simply be.

Don't let exhaustion lie to us. Don't let temporary fatigue cause permanent damage. Let our weariness take us to the throne, not the timeline.

"My flesh and my heart may fail, but God is the strength of my heart and my portion forever." —Psalm 73:26 (NIV)

God is still with us. He still restores. And we're stronger than we feel.

Reflection Questions:

1. Where have you been pouring out from an empty place—emotionally, spiritually, or mentally?
2. What expectations or pressures might you need to release to experience peace again?
3. How can you invite rest without retreating?

Lesson 9

Fighting For Peace At Home

Let's look at what's happening around us. We can see that marriage is under attack, not just from infidelity or scandal, but from distractions, unrealistic expectations, resentment, silence, and people who have no business speaking into our homes.

And if we're not intentional about protecting our marriage, we'll wake up one day and wonder how love slipped out the back door while we were distracted in the front.

We guard what we value. And if we say we value our marriage, our actions have to reflect that.

Everything Doesn't Deserve Access

One of the most dangerous things a wife can do is leave her marriage emotionally unlocked. That looks like gossiping about our husbands to people who don't pray for them. It appears that inviting opinions into our sacred space that aren't rooted in truth, wisdom, or God's guidance.

We might tell ourselves, "I'm just venting." But what we're really doing is giving outsiders keys to rooms they were never meant to walk through.

The enemy doesn't have to kick the door in when we've already left it cracked. So, close it. Lock it. Guard it.

"Above all else, guard your heart, for everything you do flows from it." —Proverbs 4:23 (NIV)

Our heart is the gate. And our home flows from it.

It starts small—sharing our frustrations with so-called friends who never respected our marriage in the first place. A few *'I can't believe he...'* texts. A lot of agreement but zero accountability. Before long, we've built a safe space for resentment—not restoration.

Every Home Has to Be Fought For

Just because we're married doesn't mean we're automatically covered. Every good thing has to be maintained, checked, and protected. And that includes our home.

Guarding our house doesn't always mean fighting others. Sometimes, it means fighting our own need to control. Our fear. Our frustration. Our insecurity.

It means asking, *"Am I making this house a home, or a war zone?"*

There were seasons when I didn't realize I was the one tearing us down—not with my hands, but with my words. With my attitude. With my silence.

We can't guard the house if our energy keeps setting it on fire.

Guarding Isn't Controlling—It's Covering

This isn't about being possessive. It's about being prayerful.

We're not trying to dominate his every move. We're asking God to cover the places we can't see. To block what we don't even know is coming.

It's spiritual. It's strategic. It's surrender.

We guard by praying over his peace.

- We guard by checking our pride at the door.
- We guard by being careful with who and what we let into our conversations, our thoughts, and our circle.

Our Marriage Is a Target

The closer we get to our purpose, the harder the hits come. Because a kingdom marriage is a threat to the enemy. When we and our husbands are in sync, we're dangerous. We're powerful. And we're covered.

So, of course, hell will send division. Distraction. Drought. Delay.

But we weren't called to crumble. We were called to cover.

"Though one may be overpowered, two can defend themselves. A cord of three strands is not quickly broken."
—Ecclesiastes 4:12 (NIV)

That third strand? That's God. Keep Him in the middle. Keep Him involved. Keep Him first.

Don't Just React—Respond Spiritually

There will be moments that test our patience. Our grace. Our sanity.

Sometimes, guarding our house means holding our tongue. At other times, it means using our voices in prayer instead of being petty.

I've learned not to respond to every jab. Every cold shoulder. Every bad mood.

I've learned my husband's many faces and am very familiar with his temperament. As a result, I've created my own counter-reactions and, if necessary, responses. Every response costs energy—and I'd rather invest mine into healing than arguing.

Guarding means learning what to ignore, what to address, and what to give to God before we open our mouths.

It's Not Paranoia—It's Protection

If something threatens our peace, our unity, or our intimacy, we're allowed to shut it down.

That includes:

- Unchecked friendships that sow division.
- Overbearing family members who refuse boundaries.
- Social media habits that feed comparison instead of connection.
- Our own habits leave no room for intimacy or communication.

Guarding the house means protecting what we're building from everything trying to break in—or break it down.

We Are Not Alone

If any of us are feeling overwhelmed, take heart. We're not the only wives who've felt like the glue, the guard, and the only ones paying attention.

We're not weak for feeling tired. We're not crazy for wanting to protect what we prayed for.

We are strong because we show up. We are wise because we see what others miss. And we're covered—because God guards those who guard what He gave them.

Reflection Questions:

1. What doors have you left cracked in your marriage—emotionally, spiritually, or relationally?
2. How can you become more intentional about protecting the peace in your home?
3. What boundaries need to be strengthened to keep outside voices from weakening your foundation?

Lesson 10

How Do We Build One Home From Two Lives?

Let's talk about something real: when you say, "I do," we're not just marrying our man. We're marrying his habits, his history, and, yes, his family.

And he's marrying ours, too. That part doesn't get enough attention. But for our marriage to thrive, we've to figure out how to leave, cleave, and build something new— together.

The transition into marriage doesn't come with an off switch for mama's opinions or daddy's expectations.

Our family may want the daughter who used to drop everything to come running, and his family might miss the son who did everything for everybody whenever they needed it and stayed quiet about it.

But now? Now he's, my husband. I'm his wife. And together, we're building our own house—not recreating theirs.

We will feel the pull. The guilt. The tension. When holidays come around. When parenting decisions clash with what our mama did. When he tells us his family thinks we've changed—and he doesn't know what to say.

We'll feel like we're being torn apart, trying to keep everyone happy. But peace doesn't live in people-pleasing. It lives in prioritizing the covenant.

For us, it appeared shortly after we got married. My dad expected me to come home for the holidays, and his family expected him to stay and celebrate with them. But we'd promised each other the holidays would look different now.

Saying no felt like a betrayal. But saying yes would've cost us the peace we were finally building.

"Therefore, shall a man leave his father and his mother and cleave unto his wife; and they shall become one flesh."—Genesis 2:24 (KJV)

Leaving isn't always physical. It's emotional. It's about loyalty. It's about knowing where your first allegiance now lies. Not to abandon your family—but to establish a new order.

Boundaries are not betrayal. They're bridges that keep everyone safe. We can love our people and still say, *"That doesn't work for our home."*

We can honor our parents and still choose a different path than they did. This isn't rebellion—it's responsibility. It's maturity. It's spiritual alignment.

Don't just expect him to set the boundaries we're unwilling to set. If we're shutting down his mama but ignoring our own overreach, that's not partnership—it's a power play. Don't do it.

We can't expect our husbands to check their people while we stay silent with ours. Mutual respect. Mutual effort. Mutual growth.

Being his wife doesn't mean replacing his mother. And him being our husband doesn't mean becoming our dad. We don't marry our parents—we marry people. People with flaws, fears, and their own way of doing life.

Our job is not to mold him into the man our daddy was—it's to love the man he's becoming. And to give him space to lead in a way that honors God, not our family's preferences.

This journey requires constant communication. Grace. And unity. It's about knowing when to speak up and when to step back. When to let our spouse handle their side, and when to stand together.

Unity doesn't mean uniformity—it means agreement in the direction we're building.

When our families pull on us, remember what we're building. A new legacy. A house that reflects both of us, not a replica of the past. Our home should be the safest place for both of us to be honest, vulnerable, and aligned.

That kind of home takes work, boundaries, and an unwavering commitment to protect what matters most—each other.

Reflection Questions:

1. Where have you struggled to establish boundaries with family in your marriage?
2. Are you expecting your spouse to enforce limits you're not upholding on your end?
3. What does unity look like in your marriage when outside voices get loud?

Lesson 11

Who Is This Man I Married?

Initially, everyone puts forth their best effort.

We show up dressed in our best, clean, intentional, thoughtful, smelling oh so good, saying all the right things—sometimes rehearsed.

Is this deceptive? Not really. It's just human nature. We want to make the best impression.

What happens when the versions of the men we married suddenly change?

The conversations instantly become shorter, the compliments become less frequent, and the small things we once adored about them…start feeling like ancient memories instead of patterns.

We ask:

What happened! Did I fall in love with who I thought he was—or…who he wanted me to believe he was.

It's not a question of judgment.

The shock leaves us wondering if, for the first time, we're finally seeing them clearly.

And if we were honest with ourselves, most of us don't usually marry the real person when standing at the altar. They typically show up later; we both do.

We're marrying representatives.

I remember noticing the first shift—not a massive one, just a silence where laughter used to be. The version I fell in love with started to fade, and the real man began to emerge.

The Representative Always Shows Up First

The representative is polished.

He listens more, tries harder, and leads with his strongest attributes.

This isn't always done by manipulation. In the early stages of love, we are all performing. We highlight what we want to be noticed and hide what we want to protect, what we're not ready to show.

So… we're both falling for the best parts of one another.

Right?

Eventually, when real life settles in, conflict arises, and the comfortable feeling we've become accustomed to replaces our performances. The masks come off.

And now we're no longer dating our potential.

We're waking up next to strangers and their patterns.

Seeing Clearly Doesn't Mean We Chose Wrong

It can be disorienting to realize the men we married aren't who we initially thought they were.

However, that doesn't mean we've made a mistake or got it wrong.

It means the real relationship has finally started.

The representative fades—and the man underneath is now exposed:

His fears

- His unhealed places
- His emotional blind spots
- His habits, not just his highlight reel

And the truth is—we're not the same women we were when they met us.

We had representatives, too.

Maybe she was more agreeable, hid her wounds, or smiled through things she can't ignore now.

This isn't failure.

It's just the next layer. And it requires real grace.

The Shock of Disappointment Is a Crossroad

The moment we realize the man we're married to isn't the one we imagined is sacred.

It's a turning point.

We can either:

- Try to turn them back into the versions we fell in love with
- Feel resentment towards them for not being who we want them to be
- Or let God teach us how to love them as they truly are—flaws, fullness, and more

This is where fantasy ends, and faithful love begins.

What's Underneath the Mask Matters More

Sometimes, the real man underneath the representative is better than we thought.

- He's not as charming, but he's solid.
- He's not as smooth, but he's sincere.
- He's not as polished, but he's present.

At other times, what's underneath reveals wounds that need healing, habits that require confrontation, and emotional immaturity that won't subside by simply praying it away.

This is where discernment is key.

Because love can't survive long-term on potential.

It needs progress.

"Wisdom is the principal thing; therefore, get wisdom: and with all thy getting get understanding." —Proverbs 4:7 (KJV)

Understanding gives us clarity—not just about who he is but about how God calls us to love and lead ourselves in it.

We're Not Responsible for His Growth—But We Are Responsible for Our Response

Once we've seen the real him, our role changes.

We're no longer responding to who he pretends to be.

We're responding to who he is right now.

That doesn't mean tolerating disrespect.

It doesn't mean staying silent when something needs to be confronted.

It means facing the truth with grace and boundaries.

We can say:

- "I love you, but this can't stay the same."
- "I see where you're hurting, and I want to support your growth—not carry it for you."
- "I'm not going to punish you for not being perfect. But I'm also not going to pretend everything's okay when it's not."

That's not control. That's clarity.

God Uses the "Real" to Grow Both of Us

When the representative fades, what remains is the raw material that God will use to shape us both.

This is where:

- Real forgiveness is needed
- Real patience is tested

- Real communication is practiced
- Real surrender is required

With God in the center, that raw material can be transformed into something more substantial than the promised performance.

"My grace is sufficient for you, for my power is made perfect in weakness." — 2 Corinthians 12:9 (NIV)

That includes the weaknesses we now see in our spouse and ourselves.

Rebuilding with Reality

We no longer need the representative.

We need honest men who are transparent enough to say, "*Here I am*," and the grace to meet him there.

Together, we can:

- Build trust slowly and intentionally
- Celebrate honesty over image
- Grow in emotional safety, not performance
- Develop spiritual maturity, one prayer at a time

Real love isn't afraid of the truth.

It builds with it.

Reflection Questions:

1. What expectations or illusions about your partner might you need to let go of?

2. Are you responding to the real version of your spouse—or still reacting to who you thought he'd be?
3. How can you love and support your partner's growth without trying to fix or control them?

Lesson 12

Married, But Lonely

It's never discussed at bridal showers or on anniversary posts.

But…most of us know it's real.

We can be married, and yet we still feel alone.

Loneliness doesn't stem from being physically distant but rather from being emotionally disconnected.

We can sit on the same couch, sleep in the same bed, and go through our daily routines together, yet this distance keeps our hearts miles apart.

This is one of the most silent struggles marriages face.

And unfortunately, it's one of the most common.

Loneliness Isn't Always About Presence—It's About Connection

Loneliness isn't just about being alone.

It's about us feeling unseen.

We may still do things together, such as sharing breakfast, attending family and friend functions, and even going to church.

Yet deep inside, we have this gnawing feeling:

I don't think he really knows me anymore.

We used to talk about everything. But…now, we just talk about bills and schedules.

I miss laughing with him, running as he chased me around the house, being listened to, and feeling a sense of connection with him.

And maybe we've tried to tell them, but we can't.

Or we're no longer trying because a part of us feels like what's the point. Nothing will change.

God Sees What Feels Invisible

God sees us when our hearts feel heavy, and our voices feel unheard.

"You have searched me, Lord, and you know me. You know when I sit and when I rise; you perceive my thoughts from afar." —Psalm 139:1–2 (NIV)

God doesn't just see the loneliness—He feels it with us.

- We're not invisible.
- We're not forgotten.

And…this season of disconnect is not the end.

The Causes of Loneliness in Marriage

Loneliness doesn't happen all at once.

It builds slowly, often from unspoken hurts or unresolved transitions.

Some of the most common causes:

- Life transitions: kids, careers, grief, or health changes
- Unmet expectations: emotional, physical, or spiritual
- Avoidance of hard conversations
- Busyness: life becomes logistics instead of intimacy
- Disconnection from God—as individuals and as a couple

None of these mean the marriage is doomed.

But they signal that something needs attention, honesty, and transparency.

We Were Made for Connection

God didn't just design marriage for partnership—He created it for closeness.

"And they were both naked, the man and his wife, and were not ashamed."— Genesis 2:25 (KJV)

That verse speaks to physical intimacy and emotional transparency—a closeness so secure that neither of us feels the need to hide.

When that connection fades, so does the sense of safety.

But the good news? It can be restored.

Start With What We Can Control

- We can't force a connection.
- We can't demand intimacy.

But…we can choose to show up with courage and vulnerability.

Start here:

- Pray for our spouses—not just about them.
- Ask God to soften both our hearts and open doors for real conversation.
- Initiate moments of closeness.

Not big gestures. Just eye contact. Affection. Listening. A question that goes deeper than "How was your day?"

Share our needs with clarity, not blame.

Try, "I miss us. I want to feel close to you again," instead of "You never talk to me anymore."

Small steps toward honesty can reopen what silence shuts down.

We're Not Failing—We're Human

Loneliness doesn't mean we're married to the wrong man.

It doesn't mean we're too needy.

It doesn't mean something's broken beyond repair.

It means we're craving what we were made for:

Closeness. Connection. Companionship.

And that longing is not shameful—it's sacred.

Even Jesus, in His darkest hour, longed for companionship.

"Then he said to them, 'My soul is overwhelmed with sorrow… Stay here and keep watch with me.'" —Matthew 26:38 (NIV)

If the Son of God could say, "I don't want to be alone right now," then so can we.

If He Doesn't Respond

We may be reading this with a knot in our stomachs—because we've tried.

- We've prayed.
- We've reached out.

And it feels like we're talking to a cement wall.

Hear this: God still sees our efforts.

- We're not weak for longing for more.
- We're not wrong for grieving the gap.
- And we're not the only ones who are feeling alone.

Keep praying—not just for our marriage, but for our own hearts as well.

Surround ourselves with support, truth, and a sense of community.

And don't give up on the possibility of restoration.

God Can Reconnect What Feels Distant

God specializes in reviving what feels too far gone.

"This is what the Sovereign Lord says to these bones: I will make breath enter you, and you will come to life."—Ezekiel 37:5 (NIV)

If He can breathe life into dry bones, He can breathe life into a dry marriage, weary hearts, and emotional walls that feel too thick to break.

But that revival often starts with humility.

With one person saying, "I miss us."

And another person choosing to lean in—even just a little.

That's all it takes to begin again.

Reflection Questions:

1. Are there areas in your marriage where emotional connection has faded?
2. What honest conversation have you been avoiding out of fear or fatigue?
3. How can you create space this week for closeness—with your spouse and God?

Lesson 13

When To Speak — And When to Stay Silent

How many of us are familiar with this saying? "Love and pride cannot grow in the same soil"? I wasn't, but the thing is when I did hear it, I got it.

Pride can be a terrible thing when it clashes with love. If we're not careful, we can become so wrapped up in our pride that we lose sight of what's truly important to us and who's truly important to us.

Being right at any cost shouldn't be what we die on our swords for. When we refuse to do or say what needs to be done or said because we choose to dig our heels in, telling ourselves it's a matter of principle.

We're not fooling anyone. Not even ourselves.

Love is simple and primarily requires understanding.

Let's compare Pride to Love.

- Pride holds grudges.
- Love releases them.
- Pride builds walls.
- Love builds bridges.

Every relationship will encounter a crossroads…over… and over…and over again:

Will I choose to protect my ego, or will I prioritize preserving our connection with each other?

Our answers determine how deep and lasting our love is and can become.

The Quiet Ways Pride Shows Up

Pride isn't always loud or arrogant.

Occasionally, it's quiet and deeply rooted.

It may sound like:

- *"I don't need to apologize FIRST."*
- *"If he really cared, he should know what I need."*
- *"Why should I be the one to bend—AGAIN?"*
- *"I'll just shut down until he figures it out."*

Pride convinces us that we're weak if we allow ourselves to be vulnerable.

Keeping the upper hand is safer than being honest.

By withholding, we have the power.

But…withholding love doesn't make us strong—it causes distance between us.

Distance creates division, even when intentions start off in a good place.

Love Requires Humility

"Do nothing out of selfish ambition or vain conceit. Rather, in humility value others above yourselves, not

looking to your own interests but each of you to the interests of the others." —Philippians 2:3–4 (NIV)

That kind of love doesn't come naturally.

It requires God's help.

Because pride always wants the last word.

The last say.

The cleanest record.

But humility says, *"Even if I'm right, I'm more committed to our love than to being right or to winning."*

Pride Keeps Score. Love Keeps Showing Up.

Keeping score feels fair.

It gives us a sense of control.

It lets us feel morally superior.

But it also keeps us trapped. Trapped in this cycle of withholding.

Pride holds on to every mistake.

Love remembers every moment we chose each other despite anything else.

"Love… is not easily angered, it keeps no record of wrongs." — 1 Corinthians 13:5 (NIV)

It's not natural—it's supernatural.

It takes real spiritual maturity to release what we feel entitled to hold on to.

But it creates a freedom that's well worth the cost.

The Fight to Be "Right" Isn't Worth Losing the Relationship

- We can win the argument and still lose the connection.
- We can prove our point but end up sleeping back-to-back in silence.
- We can say, "I told you so," and push our husband further away.
- We can hold out for our version of justice and miss an opportunity to heal together.
- The goal is not to be right.
- The goal is to be whole.

Wholeness comes when both people care more about the relationship than the scoreboard.

Apologizing Isn't Losing

Pride will try to convince us that being the first to apologize means we're weak.

That if we say, "*I'm sorry*," we're conceding and giving them the power.

That if we admit our part, they'll never admit theirs.

But apology isn't weakness—it's leadership.

It sets the tone, models humility, and creates a space for the other person to respond softly.

And even if they don't?

We still win—because we've stayed true to the heart of Christ.

"…God opposes the proud but gives grace to the humble."— James 4:6 (NIV)

If we want grace to flow through our relationship, humility must be our posture.

God Opposes Pride Because It Blocks Love

Pride isolates.

- It hardens.
- It refuses to listen.

Over time, it can create a marriage where both husband and wife walk around on eggshells instead of walking together in freedom.

That's not love.

That's performance.

But where humility leads, healing follows.

Choosing Humility Doesn't Mean Ignoring Our Needs

This isn't about pretending nothing hurts.

It's not about letting issues slide to keep things smooth.

Choosing to love over pride means:

- We speak truth, but with tenderness
- We express our needs but without manipulation
- We create space for hard conversations but with grace
- We drop our defenses, not our dignity

Knowing that love grows best in hearts that stay soft—even when it feels uncomfortable.

Letting God Deal with Their Heart While He Refines Ours

The hardest part about pride is that sometimes we feel like we're doing all the work.

We humble ourselves. We give grace. We show up, honestly.

And it feels like they're still stuck in their ego.

That's when we have to trust God to deal with their heart—while He continues to shape ours.

"If it is possible, as far as it depends on you, live at peace with everyone."— Romans 12:18 (NIV)

- We're not responsible for their growth.
- We're responsible for our response.
- Keep choosing peace.
- Keep choosing love.
- Keep choosing humility over ego.

Because that's how love endures.

Reflection Questions:

1. Where has pride been showing up in your relationship—in obvious or subtle ways?
2. What would it look like to let go of being "right" to move towards a stronger connection?
3. Is there a conversation, apology, or gesture you've resisted because pride is standing in the way?

Lesson 14

Am I Still *That Girl*?

Keeping Our Spark Alive When Life Tries to Snuff It Out

We used to laugh with our whole chest—mouth open, unbothered.

Back then, some of us would wear our husband's favorite shirt and nothing else. We'd love to tease them just because it was Tuesday or any other day.

We could turn a grocery store run into a spontaneous date just because we craved his closeness.

But somewhere between the late-night feedings, work deadlines, or the silent tension that stemmed from an argument neither of us wanted or felt like revisiting, we — the original girl —started to fade.

Not vanish—just fade.

Now, we might find ourselves looking in the mirror and sometimes wondering,

- *"What happened to her?"*
- *"Where did she go?"*
- And *"Why does this woman staring back at me feel more worn than wanted?"*

Life has a way of piling weight on top of us, the women we once were.

Not because we stopped loving—but because we started surviving.

She Didn't Disappear. She Got Buried.

I used to think that the girl I once was had died—the bold, free-spirited one who flirted without overthinking and didn't need an occasion to feel sexy.

But she didn't die.

She got lost in schedules, sacrifices, and showing up for everyone else.

Every wife has her version of this story.

Some were raising kids, some navigated illness, some chased careers, and others were simply tired from carrying the emotional weight of it all.

It's not that the love she had was gone—it's that exhaustion made room for autopilot.

But here's what I know now: that girl is still in there.

The one he fell for—the one who knew how to make his heart race—she's not gone. She never left.

She's quiet. But not dead.

Sometimes, she just needs permission to come back.

He Misses Her, Even When He Doesn't Say It

This isn't all on us.

Men change, too.

He used to be more playful. We used to call just to hear our voices.

Now, half the time, he'll come into the room but seem to be somewhere else entirely—buried in stress or some other distraction.

But if we look, we'll notice he misses "us," too.

The woman who made him feel alive.

The one who would gently rub her hand against his in public, not just out of routine but out of desire.

The one who used to ask about his dreams—not just what time the kids had practice.

Sometimes, men don't say they miss her—they just try to function without her.

They go silent. Or numb. Or become irritable.

Not because they've stopped loving us but because they don't know how to fix what feels like what quietly slipped away.

Bringing Her Back Without Losing Who We've Become

We're not supposed to be the same women we were when we first married.

Growth doesn't mean loss.

It means there's more of us now. More wisdom. More strength. More substance.

But that doesn't mean we can't bring some of her back.

The spark. The freedom. The curiosity. And especially…the laughter.

It won't look the same—but it can be even better.

Now, it's not about impressing him. It's about inviting him back into the parts of us he hasn't seen in a while.

It starts small:

- Sitting beside him instead of opposite ends of the couch.
- Sending a text that's more flirty than functional.

Playing music while we cook and dancing like nobody's watching—even if it's just him.

- It doesn't require a getaway or a grand gesture.
- It requires permission—to feel again, to pursue him again, to want to be wanted again.

And don't wait for him to initiate it all.

Be brave enough to go first.

Let God In—Because We Can't Do This Alone

Restoring passion isn't just a physical thing—it's a profoundly spiritual experience.

Sometimes, the issue isn't in the bedroom—it's in the heart.

- You're worn out.
- You've grown numb.
- You've started believing that this is just what long-term love becomes: steady but sterile.

But God didn't design love to be lukewarm.

- He made a covenant. And He made fire.
- He made intimacy that renews and laughter that heals.

Ask Him to help you remember.

Ask Him to show you how to reconnect—not just with your husband but with yourself.

"He restores my soul." —Psalm 23:3 (NIV)

Restoration doesn't always look like fireworks.

- Sometimes, it looks like a long hug that neither of us rushes.
- Sometimes, it's a late-night talk after the kids are asleep, and we both finally exhale.
- Sometimes, it's crying together because we both realize we've been drifting and no longer want to do it.

That's sacred. That's revival. That's still being that girl.

Reflection Questions

1. Where have I noticed myself pulling away emotionally or physically—and why?

2. What would bringing "that girl" back look like in this season of life—not who I used to be, but who I still am deep down?
3. How can I invite my husband into that rediscovery, and what role might God want to play in restoring us both?

Lesson 15

What Makes Him Feel Safe With Me?

There was a time when I didn't understand the weight a man carried when he walked through the front door.

I assumed that if he was quiet, something was wrong. If he wasn't opening up or appeared to have shut down, he didn't trust me enough with whatever was troubling him. Or maybe…he simply didn't care. If his energy didn't match mine, a part of him might have been pulling away.

But after many years and much prayer—I took an honest look at what I'd closed my eyes to—I'd learned something interesting: Unbeknownst to many of us, as women, we have the ability and power to set the tone of our homes.

Whether we create an atmosphere of rest or resistance, it has never been about perfection; it is more about presence.

We Can't Be His Peace If We're Always in Pieces

If we're not grounded in God, some of us may look to our mates as our source. Our emotional regulator. Our therapist. Our savior.

And when they cannot be just that …we decide to make them the villains.

That's not fair …nor has it been their role. It's God's.

When I learned to bring my emotions to God first, I stopped unloading everything on my husband's shoulders that he couldn't fix or control. When I made the shift, it did more than help me—it freed him, my husband.

"God is our refuge and strength, a very present help in trouble."— Psalm 46:1 (NKJV)

I had to stop treating my husband like he was my hiding place and trust that God was and is my refuge. When I made that switch, it was only then that I could offer my husband peace instead of pressure.

Peace Isn't Passive. It's Powerful.

Many of us have confused peace with pretending. Peace doesn't mean we stop speaking up. It simply means we now speak with purpose.

It's knowing how to:

Hold grace and still stand for the truth

Stay soft without being silent

Create calm without believing we need to be in control

When peace lives in us, it flows through us. It's hard to explain, but when we know, we know.

It looks like:

- Compassionate eyes when our partner comes in later than usual
- A warm touch, even after a disagreement

- Asking, "*How can I help?*" before demanding, "*Why didn't you?*"

Let's be clear. I'm not saying we should baby our husbands. We should build them up. Complement them. Show adoration and appreciation for who they are and what they bring into our lives.

We, as women, often expect and receive compliments — little tokens of appreciation. Yet, very rarely do most husbands receive similar or, at best, glimmers of adoration in return.

Before going all female ninja warrior on me, let me explain what I mean. Realistically, if we were truly honest with ourselves. How many of us can say that showering our men with appreciation, not just sexually but also through other actions and words, lets them know how much we value their worth without reminders or prompts?

It's our job to build up our husbands. We're their BIGGEST and BEST cheerleaders. Remind them of that.

The Home Should Be His Harbor

The world hits him all day. Deadlines. Disrespect. Disappointment.

He may not tell us everything—but when he does share…listen. We shouldn't offer our opinions or divert the conversation to us unless… he's done sharing and wants to know about what we have going on. Let him know that whatever he experienced, he felt it all.

And when he steps into our presence, what does he feel? What does he hear?

Another list of what he didn't do.

Another cold shoulder because he missed our cue.

Another mental chess match just to prove he loves us.

Or does he feel like he can exhale? Fall apart a little? Lay his burdens down for just a moment?

"Better to live on a corner of the roof than share a house with a quarrelsome wife." —*Proverbs 21:9 (NIV)*

If I could be honest, this verse previously offended me—until I realized I had been her before. And I can own that I realized she wasn't the wife I wanted to be.

I made my frustration louder than my faith. My attitude was sharper than my support. My presence was harder than the peace he needed and deserved. I needed to change...for me and for us.

Being His Peace Isn't About Shrinking—It's About Stewardship

We're not doormats. We're gatekeepers.

With that comes power.

We get to decide what atmosphere we want to create in our homes.

- Do we invite the Holy Spirit in or host hostility?
- Do our words heal, or do they haunt him?
- Does our presence comfort or convict?

It took me time, guidance, and a lot of prayer to understand that gentleness wasn't weakness—but wisdom wrapped in power.

"A gentle answer turns away wrath, but a harsh word stirs up anger." —Proverbs 15:1 (NIV)

My harsh words weren't just stirring up arguments—they were stirring up anxiety in a man already at war outside our home.

We Don't Need a Perfect Man to Be a Peaceful Wife

This isn't about ignoring red flags or enabling emotional laziness.

This is about creating a culture of connection where love doesn't have to scream to be heard.

Sometimes, he'll miss it.

Sometimes, we'll feel lonely.

Sometimes, our effort won't be reciprocated in the moment.

But when we are led by the Spirit instead of our mood? We shift atmospheres. We disarm egos, both his and ours. We nurture trust.

And when he sees that home is where his heart is safe? He returns to us. Again, and again. Not out of duty—but desire.

Peace Begins With Surrender

I learned this lesson the hard way.

I couldn't pray for peace in our home while sowing sarcasm. I couldn't speak Proverbs 31 while living like Proverbs 21.

Peace wasn't a prayer; I prayed for him. It was a posture I chose with God.

And slowly, it shifted things. My husband softened. I quieted. We connected.

Reflection Questions:

1. What energy or emotional climate do you typically bring into your home?
2. Are there areas where you've unknowingly become more pressure than peace?
3. What would it look like to offer emotional safety before expecting emotional availability?

Lesson 16

Submission Isn't A Dirty Word

"I'll submit when he acts like a man worth following."

I've heard those words more times than I can count. Not just from strangers or women on social media—but from girlfriends, cousins, and other women I love and respect. And truthfully, I got it.

At one time, the word submission would make me flinch when I heard it. It felt as if I were losing myself, shrinking to fit a version of womanhood that didn't match my strength.

But as I grew in my marriage and in my walk with God, I've learned that submission isn't about shrinking—it's about surrendering the right way, to the right person, for the right purpose.

The world's definition of submission is often interpreted as silence, weakness, or relinquishing our voices and our strength to men who, on a good day, might have no idea what to do with it. But the bible has shown me something completely different about it.

According to the Word, submission is mutual, honoring God and building trust, not fear. And when done well, it creates a marriage that can endure far more than just the good days.

What Submission Is (and Isn't)

Submission is not silence. It's not slavery. It's not spiritual manipulation or control disguised in church attire. It's not compliance out of fear. It's not disappearing so our husbands can feel like they're the big men in charge.

Submission is about order, trust, and mutual deference.

"Submit to one another out of reverence for Christ." — Ephesians 5:21 (NIV)

Yes—one another. That means man must submit, too, not to our authority but to God's. His role is sacrificial leadership. Ours is trusting God enough to follow even when it's hard.

If that sounds like a lot, it is. But it's holy work. It's not something we do because our husbands always get it right. It's something we do because we trust the God who does.

I Thought I Was Leading with Wisdom

I used to lead with facts, spreadsheets, bullet point presentations, and logic. Even with all that support, I had to learn that believing my way was the "right" one, in my spirit, I knew I could be wrong.

Finances were one of the main topics of discussion early on in my marriage. My husband and I were discussing a financial challenge, and each of us had very different opinions on how we should handle it.

I'd done the research, did the math, and came ready to the discussion with all of my facts. My husband listened to my case, paused, and then simply shared that he wanted to do something different. Everything in me wanted to scream.

"But…"

If you're anything like I was, you'd want to throw a fit and reiterate the proof that supported your case until either he conceded to my way of thinking or was shut down and did what he wanted to do anyway.

Instead, I paused, exhaled, said a silent prayer, then…Let it go. "Okay… we'll do it your way," I responded. My response wasn't sarcastic, nor did I give him a side-eye. I meant it.

You'll never believe what happened next. My husband seemed relieved, and he stood taller.

He took ownership of the situation and handled it. He was so sexy to me in that moment. Something seemed as if it had changed in him. This was my guy, all authoritative, the one I fell in love with and knew I married. I stopped trying to figure things out for us.

Mutual Surrender Is Built to Last

Submission isn't about erasing ourselves. It's about giving up control—when it's safe when it's right when it's led by God. That's what mutual surrender is: each of us bringing our whole selves and laying them down, not because we're weak, but because we're both committed to something bigger than our own pride.

The result? A marriage that isn't just built on individual feelings but on faith.

What Keeps Marriages Going Isn't Excitement—It's Endurance

Nobody talks about the boredom. The routine when a marriage starts to feel more like a task list than a baby come close event. The passion fades.

One day, we could look up and realize how long it's been since we've laughed, touched, or even looked at one another with that "ooh baby" look that makes our knees go weak.

Built-to-last love isn't built on butterflies. It's built on decisions. Forgiveness. Grace when it's not deserved. Showing up when you feel spent. Choosing joy when monotony dulls everything around you.

You don't fall into lasting love. You build it—with prayer, humility, and staying power.

Control Kills Connection

One of the biggest roadblocks to lasting intimacy? Control.

I hate to admit it, but I used to measure everything—which one of us apologized first the last time, who was more tired, who did more with the kids, who carried the emotional weight. I kept a scoreboard.

But God doesn't. And neither should we. Petty, right? I know…That was the old, immature me. A lot has changed since then.

Control doesn't breed safety. It breeds resentment. When I learned to release my grip, everything softened. My husband's heart. My heart. Our rhythm. It took trust. And it took truth. But it also made me remember. I wasn't the Holy Spirit in his life—I was his helper, not his handler.

Love That Evolves With Us

We're not the same women our husbands married. And they aren't the same men we married. We both are evolving—becoming new versions of ourselves, year by year. And that's a good thing.

But evolution without communication causes erosion.

Marriage isn't maintenance—it's movement. We have to stay curious. Keep asking. Keep learning. Keep leaning in.

Let God Be the Glue

When everything else cracked—expectations, routines, our understanding of each other—it was God who kept it from shattering.

There were times I prayed for God to fix my husband. But He started with me. My perspective. My posture. My pride. And once He had my heart, everything else fell into place.

We were built differently—not because we were perfect, but because we were surrendered. And when that became OUR foundation...no storm could shake us.

Reflection Questions

1. What lessons or wounds shaped how you view submission?
2. Where might your need for control be rooted in fear, not faith?
3. What does mutual surrender look like in your relationship today?
4. What routines or habits can you shift to fight for joy and endurance?

5. How has God used uncomfortable seasons to deepen—not destroy—your connection?

Lesson 17

What Happened To The Flame?

We were lying next to each other like strangers. I missed him—but didn't know how to say it. Then, one night, I turned to him, touched his hand, and said, 'I miss us.' That was the spark. It was not a grand gesture—just a crack in the distance we'd built.

Falling in love is easy. Staying in love? That takes intentional effort.

In the beginning, it's butterflies and late-night conversations. However, over time, routines tend to take over. Work piles up. The kids need everything. Our energy feels stretched thin.

And before we realize it, romance has become a memory, not a moment.

Realistically, passion doesn't just disappear—it gets buried under neglect.

And anything buried can be revived with care.

Romance Is a Choice, Not a Phase

Romance isn't a feeling that visits us—it's a rhythm we cultivate.

It doesn't flourish by accident. It grows with intention.

There will be dry seasons:

- When stress hits hard
- When emotions are thin
- When nothing feels exciting

But love that is tended to won't wither in the drought.

"Many waters cannot quench love; rivers cannot sweep it away." — Song of Solomon 8:7 (NIV)

That's the love we're fighting for: not a spark that flickers, but a flame that survives storms.

Connection Runs Deeper Than Touch

Intimacy is more than physical—it's emotional.

When the connection feels distant, don't start with candles and outfits. Start with curiosity.

- Ask: What have you been carrying on your own?
- Ask: What used to make you feel seen and pursued?
- Ask: How can I love you better this week?

Reconnecting starts with presence—not performance.

Love Requires Maintenance

Love is like a fire. It doesn't die out in a moment. But left untended? It cools.

- Date nights aren't extra—they're anchors.
- Thoughtful gestures aren't small—they're sacred.
- Flirting isn't just for dating—it's fuel.

We don't need grand romantic gestures. We need intentional moments.

Don't Ignore the Drift

Many couples don't break because of a significant issue—they drift due to consistent inattention.

- Texts get shorter.
- Conversations get shallow.
- Laughter gets rare.

"You have forsaken the love you had at first. Consider how far you have fallen! Repent and do the things you did at first." — Revelation 2:4–5 (NIV)

Sometimes, the path forward is a return:

- Return to laughter.
- Return to compliments.
- Return to pursuit.

Pursuit Doesn't Have to Be Pricey—Just Present

Here are simple but powerful ways to turn toward each other again:

- Pray together—even if it's an awkward moment.
- Leave a voice memo that says, "*I'm thinking of you.*"
- Hide a note where they can easily find it.
- Touch more. Smile more. Speak with intention.
- Be the person they used to love talking to.

These habits are holy. They nurture the connection that time, and tasks try to bury.

When We're the Only One Trying

If the effort feels one-sided, don't give up. And don't grow bitter.

Take it to God first. Then, bring it to your spouse with grace and clarity—not guilt or blame.

"Let us not become weary in doing good, for at the proper time we will reap a harvest if we do not give up." — Galatians 6:9 (NIV)

Keep showing love. Keep leading by example. And when needed, have the hard conversations that honor truth over resentment.

Spiritual Intimacy Fuels Emotional Intimacy

There's nothing more magnetic than praying with someone we love.

When God is at the center, connection becomes easier.

- Pray together regularly.
- Share what God is teaching you.
- Read scripture out loud before bed.

"A triple-braided cord is not easily broken." — Ecclesiastes 4:12 (NLT)

Let God braid your hearts back together—again and again.

We Can Reignite What Life Has Dimmed

We weren't created to live on autopilot. And we don't have to settle for a roommate with a ring.

Yes, love evolves. But it should never evaporate.

When two people choose each other again—and again—and again? Even the spark that faded can burn deeper.

It's not about going back to what we had. It's about becoming something even stronger.

Reflection Questions:

1. Have you been prioritizing your partner the way you did in the beginning?
2. What small action can you take this week to spark intentional intimacy?
3. In what area do you need God's help to soften your heart and renew your pursuit of one another?

Lesson 18

Still Here. Still Fighting. Still Us.

If we wanted to be honest, we'd admit we're not the same women we were a year ago. And our husbands, they aren't the same men they were this time last year either.

But…what happens when our growth feels out of sync? When we're evolving, and our husbands feel stuck. Or when life shifts us both into different lanes and the connection that once felt natural now feels… forced.

Here's the truth: Not all distance in marriage comes from drama. Sometimes, it just comes from drift.

The conversations turn shallow. The laughter gets quiet. We're living together, but not walking together.

But here's the good news: Change doesn't have to divide us. When handled with grace and intention, it can deepen our bond.

Change Isn't the Enemy. Stagnation Is.

Love doesn't mean staying the same. It means learning to grow with someone, even if the journey takes a different path.

Growth becomes dangerous when:

- One person grows, and the other stays passive.
- Both grow but in silence.

It's not the growth that hurts. It's the unshared growth that widens the gap.

We don't have to grow in perfect sync. We just have to stay committed to growing together.

Alignment Matters More Than Affection

We can love someone deeply and still be drifting apart.

Love is the foundation, but alignment builds the future:

- **Spiritually**: Are we still walking toward the same purpose?
- **Emotionally**: Are we staying curious about each other?
- **Practically**: Are our lives still working in a way that nurtures closeness?

"Can two walk together, except they be agreed?" — Amos 3:3 (KJV)

We don't need to be the same. We need to be committed to connection.

Spot the Subtle Drift

Emotional distance rarely comes in one big moment. It shows up slowly:

- Less eye contact.
- Avoiding hard conversations.
- Separate goals, separate screens, separate lives.

These aren't deal-breakers. They're check-engine lights.

When does the connection start to fade? Fight for it early.

Ask the Hard Questions

Growth isn't just personal. In marriage, it's relational.

Check-in with each other. Check-in with ourselves.

Ask:

- What's changing in me that I haven't expressed?
- What's shifting in him that I haven't made space to support?
- What are we building—on purpose or by default?

The more we understand each other, the easier it is to stay aligned.

Grow in Grace, Not Just Goals

One of us may be growing faster—spiritually, emotionally, mentally.

Don't let that breed pride. And don't let it breed shame.

"May the God who gives endurance and encouragement give you the same attitude of mind toward each other…"
— Romans 15:5-6 (NIV)

This is about unity. Not uniformity.

We can be in different places as long as we're still walking in the same direction.

Stay Curious

The versions of the spouses we married aren't the final versions of them.

Ask new questions. Create new dreams. Check-in with fresh eyes.

Ask:

- What's something new you're hoping for?
- What's been heavy for you lately?
- What has God been showing you recently?

Curiosity is how connection stays alive.

Make Growth a Shared Value

Growing together doesn't mean doing everything the same way. It means celebrating each other's evolution while staying emotionally connected.

- Read something together.
- Set a shared goal.
- Pray into each other's next chapter.
- Dream out loud about what we want to become.

Let growth be sacred ground, not a silent struggle.

If He's Not Growing Like We Are

We can't drag our husbands into maturity. That's not our job. However, what we can do is inspire them with our example of grace.

- Keep praying.
- Keep showing up with integrity.
- Keep inviting, not controlling.

"Let us not become weary in doing good... for at the proper time, we will reap a harvest if we do not give up."
— *Galatians 6:9 (NIV)*

Our love can plant seeds. And in time, it can produce fruit.

Together Is a Daily Choice

We don't grow together by accident. We do it by choosing each other again and again.

Even when it's hard. Even when we're tired. Even when it would be easier to just coast.

Choose:

- Intentional check-ins.
- Prayers over our marriage.
- Celebrating small wins.
- Protecting time for authentic connection.

When we choose together, even the rough seasons can become sacred ground.

Reflection Questions:

1. Are you and your spouse growing together—or just side by side?
2. What conversations or moments could you initiate this week to rebuild emotional closeness?
3. How can you support his growth while staying accountable to your own?

Lesson 19

When He Shuts Down

Conflict is not the enemy of love. Avoidance is. Silence is. Bitterness is.

The truth is—if we love someone and we're close to them, we will fight for them, with them, and for them.

We'll disagree. We'll disappoint each other. We'll have moments when our tone is sharp, our timing is off, and our patience wears thin.

The goal isn't to never argue. It's to argue well.

Because healthy conflict, handled with humility, respect, and care, can actually draw us closer—not push us apart.

Avoiding Conflict Doesn't Create Peace

Instead of shutting down, I told him, 'That hurt me.' No yelling. Just honesty. It didn't fix everything, but it cracked open the silence.

Avoiding conflict may feel safer in the moment.

But silence is not the same as peace.

Unspoken pain doesn't disappear. It simmers beneath the surface until a minor disagreement turns into an emotional explosion.

- One person feels unheard.
- The other feels blindsided.

And the real issue gets buried under years of unspoken tension.

True peace doesn't come from pretending everything is fine. It comes from creating a safe space where people can be honest without fear of hostility.

What Does It Mean to "Fight Fair"?

Fighting fair isn't about being passive. It's about being constructive.

It means:

- We're honest but not cruel.
- We listen as much as we speak.
- We respond instead of reacting.
- We attack the issue, not each other.
- We aim for resolution, not control.

"Everyone should be quick to listen, slow to speak and slow to become angry." — James 1:19 (NIV)

That's not just good advice—it's emotional strategy.

What Fighting Unfair Looks Like:

- Bringing up the past to win the argument.
- Weaponizing silence or sarcasm.
- Shaming or blaming.
- Refusing to listen until it's said the "right" way.
- Threatening the relationship every time things get hard.

These are not just toxic habits. They're emotional weapons. And every time they're used, trust takes a hit.

Set Conflict Boundaries Before We Need Them

We don't create rules for conflict in the middle of it. We set them when things are calm.

Try boundaries like:

- No yelling.
- No interrupting.
- No walking out without explanation.
- No name-calling.

If we take a break, we always return to resolve it.

These aren't rules to restrict. They serve as guardrails to protect the connection.

Understand Each Other's Conflict Language

Just like love languages, people fight differently as well.

Some process immediately.

Others need space to cool off.

Some want to talk it through.

Others shut down when emotions rise.

Knowing each other's wiring reduces confusion and escalations.

Ask:

- *What helps you feel safe when we disagree?*
- *What shuts you down or makes you withdraw?*
- *How can I stay present, even when it's tense?*

Pause to Reset, Not to Avoid

It's okay to pause when emotions are too high. Just don't use silence as a form of punishment.

Say:

- *"I want to handle this with love, but I need 10 minutes to reset."*
- *"Let's talk about this tonight when we're both more rested."*

Conflict isn't just about what we say. It's about how and when we say it.

Disagreement Doesn't Mean Division

It's easy to forget: our spouse is not our enemy.

Conflict can make it feel like a battle. However, the real battle is often deeper—emotional, spiritual, or unresolved.

"For our struggle is not against flesh and blood…" — Ephesians 6:12 (NIV)

When you re-frame the fight from "me vs. you" to "us vs. the problem," everything changes.

We stop proving points. We start protecting the peace.

Apologies Should Heal, Not Harm

Not all apologies bring healing. True apologies say:

- *"I was wrong."*
- *"I see how I hurt you."*
- *"Will you forgive me?"*
- *False apologies deflect responsibility:*
- *"I'm sorry you feel that way."*
- *"Well, if you hadn't…"*
- *"Fine, sorry—happy now?"*

"A gentle answer turns away wrath, but a harsh word stirs up anger."— Proverbs 15:1 (NIV)

Soft words open hearts. Defensiveness closes them.

Don't Just Move On—Grow Through It

Every argument is an opportunity to:

- Learn something new.
- Build emotional muscle.
- Practice grace.
- Deepen understanding.

Conflict is inevitable. Unresolved conflict is optional.

We don't need to fear tension. We just need tools to move through it with love, not ego.

Because marriages that grow through conflict are the ones that last.

Reflection Questions:

1. How do you typically handle conflict—and is it creating connection or causing distance?
2. What new boundaries or check-ins could help protect emotional safety during disagreements?

3. What would it look like to fight for resolution, not to win?

Lesson 20

The Tone We Set Without A Word

Most of us might believe that men don't talk. That they keep everything bottled up. But any wife who's loved a man through more than just the good days knows this: silence doesn't mean he's fine.

It doesn't mean nothing is going on. Sometimes, silence is screaming—we just have to listen a little differently to hear it.

We often expect our men to love us like we do—through verbal affirmations, deep conversations, and long texts full of feelings. But many men were taught to survive by being strong, not soft. Raised to protect, not process. They don't show emotions the same way we do. That doesn't mean they don't feel them.

And as wives, especially women who walk with God, we must stop interpreting His silence as rejection. Instead, we need to learn what that silence is actually saying.

Still Waters Run Deep

Just because he's quiet doesn't mean he's empty. That man is thinking, carrying, praying, and weighing things—usually for us, for the family. The pressure he doesn't talk about but feels every day.

He may not say it, but he's watching the bills stack up. He's wondering if he's enough. If he's doing right by us. If he's living up to expectations—even the ones we never speak on.

So no, sis—his silence isn't a lack of care. It's often the weight of it.

One of the greatest gifts we can give our husbands is space. It's not a suspicious space. Not space we fill with side-eyes and attitude. But real space—without demand, without pressure.

Let him process in peace. Let our calm be the invitation. Some of us would be surprised what a man will reveal when he knows he won't be interrogated or criticized the moment he opens up.

"The purposes of a person's heart are deep waters, but one who has insight draws them out."— Proverbs 20:5 (NIV)

Drawing out a quiet man takes insight. Wisdom. Patience. Not control. Not force. Be gentle but attentive. Because even when he's silent, something's being said.

Creating Safe Space

When a man finally opens up, it's not the time to correct him or critique his delivery. He may stumble over his words. He might not say everything perfectly. But if you cut him off or twist what he said, don't expect him to try again.

Some men have learned that silence is safer. And if we're not careful, we'll make them believe their vulnerability is a liability.

That's why safety matters more than sensitivity. Our husbands need to know that their truths—no matter how raw or rough around the edges—are safe with you.

It's not about fixing him. It's about seeing him. Hearing what he doesn't say. Catching the things in his eyes that didn't make it into words. And meeting them not with accusations but with prayer.

"A gentle answer turns away wrath, but a harsh word stirs up anger."— *Proverbs 15:1 (NIV)*

Our tone can either draw him in or drive him out. So, when he's brave enough to speak, don't turn his honesty into a debate.

His Silence Doesn't Mean He's Okay

Let's be real. Some of us only ask, "Are you okay?" because we want to hear, "Yes." We don't actually want to deal with the mess behind the "no."

But a man will keep pushing until he can no longer do so. And when that breakdown comes, it won't look like tears. It might look like distance. Frustration. Shutting down or…checking out. Pay attention.

Wives who are spiritually grounded know that the Holy Spirit often speaks before their husbands do.

So, if he's quiet for too long, ask God:

- *"What's he carrying that he doesn't have words for?"*
- *"What's the weight he's not naming, but wearing?"*
- *"And how do You want me to love him through it?"*

That's not weakness—that's wisdom.

Discernment isn't just for the prayer closet. It's for the kitchen, the bedroom, the ride home from work when our husbands haven't said a word.

Love Him Differently, Not Less

Loving a man with a quiet heart doesn't mean loving less. It means loving smarter. It's giving him the kind of support that doesn't require a performance.

Some days, the best thing we can do is sit with him in silence, our hand in his, no words—just presence.

Other times, it's praying for him in the hallway while he decompresses alone in the bedroom.

And when he finally does speak, it's listening without rehearsing our reply. It's seeing his quiet moments not as an emotional absence but as an emotional economy—he's trying to manage what he feels in a world that rarely gives him space to feel.

"Be completely humble and gentle; be patient, bearing with one another in love."— Ephesians 4:2 (NIV)

Being married to a man who doesn't always speak from the heart doesn't mean the heart isn't there; it simply means the words aren't always coming from the heart. It just means God is inviting us to love him in a way that doesn't rely on words.

Reflection Questions:

1. Have you confused your husband's silence with emotional absence?
2. How can you create a safer, softer space for him to reveal his heart to you?
3. What is God showing you about your role in drawing out your husband's inner world?

Lesson 21

Bringing Baggage To The Table

Every person brings something to the table.

Some of it is beautiful:

- Wisdom
- Loyalty
- Strength
- Faith

And some of it? It's heavy:

- Old wounds
- Fear of abandonment
- Silent vows like "*I'll never let anyone hurt me again*"

Before the vows, before the rings, long before the "I do," we packed bags we didn't even know we'd carry into our marriage.

This isn't about how we'd respond in the heat of the moment—that's coming next.

This is about what's been sitting quietly in our hearts long before our spouse ever touched a nerve.

Marriage doesn't erase the past. It reveals what we carried in.

But here's the hope: when surrendered to God, our past doesn't disqualify us. It can become the foundation for a more substantial healing and stronger love.

The Bags We Didn't Know We Packed

After our son died, I was in therapy. It wasn't until one of those sessions that I realized I wasn't angry with my husband—I was furious that our beautiful baby boy was gone. I was struggling with my own grief. I'd look into my husband's face and see our baby's eyes.

That indescribable pain pierced my heart in a way that couldn't be appeased. I withdrew from our children and even from my husband. I had questions—so did he—that would go unanswered.

At times, we clung to one another, and at other times, he'd close off and grieve alone. Though I'd done the same, I still needed him. I felt that no one could understand what we were feeling. And when he needed space, I felt deserted.

Each of us carried our own level of hurt, disappointment, and unanswered questions. We wondered if there was anything we could have done differently—but we knew we couldn't stop what God allowed to happen.

That season didn't just test our love; it revealed the deeper layers of pain I hadn't realized I carried into our marriage.

I grew up in a home where conflict was loud and sometimes violent. I never saw the physical fights, but I heard them. Shouting, banging, furniture scraping. I saw the aftermath. It made me retreat. As an adult, I didn't want the sins of my parents to become my own.

As adults, many of us expect disappointment because consistency was never modeled for us. We may choose to wear our strength like armor because softness once got our hearts hurt.

None of this began with our husbands—but it does affect them. And us. Unless we bring it into the light.

Healing doesn't require pretending. It begins by acknowledging what has hurt us and then allowing God to re-purpose it—not just remove it.

What We Survived Wasn't Wasted

That breakup that left us shattered. It made us wiser. That betrayal that stole our peace. It drew us closer and made us cling tighter to God. That trauma we thought disqualified us. It made us more empathetic, more discerning, more equipped.

"And we know that in all things God works for the good of those who love Him…"—Romans 8:28 (NIV)

All things. Not just the good days. Not just the pretty chapters. Even the nights we cried ourselves to sleep. Even the years we didn't think we'd recover.

God doesn't waste pain. He uses it to build something better with us, not despite us.

Our Past Doesn't Disqualify Us—It Deepens Us

Some women enter marriage with silent shame—things they did, things done to them, versions of themselves they'd rather forget.

But grace says: You are not what happened to you. You are what God is doing in you now.

A healed woman doesn't just love harder—she loves wiser. She's not perfect. She's present. She doesn't avoid pain. She turns pain into purpose.

Let God Take the Head of the Table

Our husbands and we may carry different pasts. Different mistakes. Different scars.

But the same God can redeem us both.

We are not our husband's savior. And he is not our healer.

But together, under God's direction, we can:

- Break generational cycles
- Build emotional and spiritual safety

Create a legacy that begins with grace

"Unless the Lord builds the house, the builders labor in vain…" — Psalm 127:1 (NIV)

We don't have to build with perfection. However, we must first create and stand on the foundation we build with God.

Bring the History. But Lead with Healing.

Our marriage doesn't need to be spotless. It just needs to be surrendered.

Show up with humility. Lead with truth. Love with intention.

Sit down at the table. Take our seat beside our husband—not because we have no past, but because we're no longer ruled by it.

We didn't survive all that just to carry it like shame. We survived it so our love could carry weight.

"But forget all that—it is nothing compared to what I am going to do. For I am about to do something new…" — *Isaiah 43:18–19 (NLT)*

Reflection Questions:

1. What pieces of your past still influence how you show up in love?
2. Where might you be carrying unhealed hurt into your current relationship?
3. How can you invite God to re-purpose your past instead of reliving it?

Lesson 22

It's Not About What Just Happened

In the last lesson, we discussed the past we brought with us—the grief, the pain, the scars, and the unspoken patterns that have shaped our view of love.

But what happens when that past shows up in the present—uninvited?

What happens when a sigh, a sharp tone, or a forgotten text brings it all flooding back?

- He didn't respond fast enough.
- She sighed a little too loud.
- He joked a little too carelessly.

Suddenly, we're not just in this moment anymore.

We're reacting to something more profound.

Something older.

Something unresolved.

That's the power of a trigger. And we need to talk about it.

It happens suddenly

We find ourselves spiraling.

Angry. Shut down. Ready to fight.

But…when we step back. We realize that this isn't really about this moment.

It's about what this moment woke up inside of us.

Old hurts. Old fears. Old rejections.

We're not just reacting to what they did. We're reacting to what it triggered.

Not Every Fight Is About the Trash

Ever felt irritated after walking into the kitchen and finding the trash bin still full, even after asking our husbands to take it out?

So, are we furious about a full bin, or is it something else?

"Be completely humble and gentle; be patient, bearing with one another in love." — Ephesians 4:2 (NIV)

It takes maturity to say:

"I'm not mad about the trash. I'm mad because I felt unheard. Again."

This level of honesty will save our marriages more than shouting matches or stone-cold silences ever will.

We All Bring Wounds We Didn't Ask For

We've already unpacked the truth: we all bring wounds we didn't ask for.

But what do we do next when those wounds get bumped? That's where healing—or harm—can begin.

Nobody chooses trauma.

It finds us through betrayal. Neglect. Absence. Broken promises.

And now, here we are—grown, in love, married, or preparing for it—still dragging invisible wounds into sacred spaces.

- We jump to conclusions.
- We lash out over "small" things.
- We shut down before anyone can abandon us first.
- We're not crazy. We're conditioned. And God wants us to unlearn that survival mode—together.

Our Spouse Isn't a Mind Reader—But They Can Be a Safe Place

Marriage won't heal triggers we refuse to name.

We can't expect them to tiptoe through our trauma without a map.

Healing isn't about making them guess. It's about making the brave choice to tell them.

Out loud. With love. Without shame.

- *"When your tone gets sharp, it reminds me of being talked down to as a kid."*
- *"When you walk away mid-conversation, it feels like abandonment."*
- *"When you joke about that, it reopens old wounds."*

Silence doesn't protect our marriage. Truth does.

Not Every Trigger Deserves a Reaction—Some Need Reflection

We don't have to swing at every emotional pitch.

Sometimes, the holiest thing you can do is pause and ask:

"Is this really about him—or is this about something God needs to heal in me?"

And sometimes, it's both.

That's okay.

We just need the wisdom to know which battles are inside of us and which ones are between us.

"The purposes of a person's heart are deep waters, but one who has insight draws them out." — Proverbs 20:5 (NIV)

Insight doesn't excuse hurt. It just keeps hurting from running the whole show.

Healing Isn't Always Instant. But It's Always Worth It.

There is no microwave healing.

Healing comes in layers:

- Through prayer.
- Through safe conversations.
- Through honest tears.
- Through intentional work.

It's not just about our healing either.

Our spouses have triggers, too.

- Sometimes that silence we're mad about. It's our husband's survival mode.
- Sometimes that defensiveness? It's his old hurt speaking up before he even realizes it.

Healing together is one of the most intimate, holy acts of marriage.

Give It to God—Then Talk It Through

Some triggers need:

- A journal.
- A counselor.
- A prayer closet.

All triggers need God.

We need to bring our broken places to Him first. Before we get them to our husbands.

"The Lord is close to the brokenhearted and saves those who are crushed in spirit." — Psalm 34:18 (NIV)

God doesn't shame us for being tender. He meets us in it.

He loves us through it. He grows us from it.

Let Him.

Then—with His grace covering us—invite our husband into that space, not to fix us, but to walk with us through it.

Triggers don't have to sabotage our connection. They can deepen it—when we're brave enough to name them and patient enough to work through them together.

Reflection Questions:

1. What arguments in your relationship seem to trigger something deeper inside you?
2. Have you named your triggers—first to yourself, then to your spouse?
3. How can you become a safe place for your spouse's triggers, too, not just your own?

Lesson 23

Being His Safe Place

Every man wants peace. But not every man finds it at home.

Some find it in their car, parked two blocks from the house. Some find it in the gym, in a video game, in long hours at work, or in conversations that never should've taken place. Not because they don't love us—but because they don't feel safe enough to breathe around us.

This may have been hard for some of us to admit. But it's real.

And as wives, if we want to be the place he runs to—not from—we've got to look at the kind of space we've created.

Where Does He Find His Peace

It's easy to assume that if he's coming home, everything's fine. But physical presence doesn't mean emotional safety. A man can sit on our couch and still be miles away in his spirit.

So…what do we do?

We ask ourselves:

- Can he exhale around me?
- Does he feel respected here?
- Do I listen—or do I lecture?

- Do I protect his flaws—or throw them back at him?

Absolute safety isn't just about being sweet when things are sweet. It's about being steady when our man is distant or when he's struggling and doesn't have the words yet.

"Her husband has full confidence in her and lacks nothing of value." — Proverbs 31:11 (NIV)

This kind of confidence doesn't show up without evidence. A safe space is built through consistency. Through covering our husbands in prayer, not controlling them through pressure.

Be His Peace, Not Another Fight

If the streets are loud, work is demanding, and every voice outside tells him he's not enough—he needs to come home to peace. Not perfection, but peace.

We don't need to have all the answers. We don't have to try and fix everything. But we do need to make space for our husbands to let go of the weight they're carrying.

Sometimes, that looks like silence—not the cold kind, but the calm kind. Sometimes, that looks like asking, *"How can I show up for you today?"* instead of, *"Why are you acting like that?"*

Being a safe space means learning to love without conditions. It means remembering that our tone matters just as much as our timing. That softness isn't weakness—it's wisdom.

"A gentle answer turns away wrath, but a harsh word stirs up anger." — Proverbs 15:1 (NIV)

Stop Competing With the World

Social media may entice him with everything possible. Every kind of woman. Every opinion. Every so-called relationship goal. And if we're not careful, we'll start performing instead of loving. Reacting instead of responding.

The truth is: the real flex isn't being the loudest, the prettiest, or the one who *"tells it like it is."* The real flex is being the one he can trust. The one who covers him when life uncovers him.

We can't control what he sees—but we can control what he feels when he's with us. And when we're his soft place to land, no post, no DM, no fantasy can compete with that reality.

Love Is a Covering

There will be days when he disappoints us. Moments where he says the wrong thing or says nothing at all. But if we respond with grace, with strength, with patience—we remind him that home isn't just a place. It's a person.

That doesn't mean we stay silent in the face of pain. It means we speak the truth in love. It means we pray more than we pout. It means we trust God to reach him in the places we can't.

Because real love covers—not to hide, but to heal.

"Above all, love each other deeply, because love covers over a multitude of sins." — 1 Peter 4:8 (NIV)

Let Him Be Vulnerable Without Regret

When he opens up—even just a little—that's not the time to correct, criticize, or compare. That's our moment to show him what safety really looks like. To show him that his softness isn't a liability. It's a bridge.

Most men were never taught how to process emotion. But they know how to feel it. And they're watching how we respond.

- Do we shut down when he shares?
- Do we punish him for his honesty?
- Or do we meet him with maturity?

The safest wives aren't perfect. But they're present. They're perceptive. And they pray like warriors for the man they love—even when he doesn't have the words.

Reflection Questions:

1. What kind of emotional atmosphere are you creating in your home?
2. In what ways have you made it hard for your husband to open up?
3. How can you respond more gently, listen more closely, and love more intentionally starting today?

Lesson 24

Touch Me Like You See Me

We're all grown folks, right? So... let's have a grown conversation. This isn't one of those where we exchange polite pleasantries or avoid discussing those hush-hush topics and are expected to "just perform our wifely duties."

Most of us have some idea of what I mean when I refer to those strict narratives that were handed down to us by the older women in our families or from those senior wives in the church; the real—the sacred—the fire that doesn't just live under the sheets but under the covenant conversations.

Sex in marriage isn't a sin, nor should it be looked upon as a wifely chore. It's not something to be checked off or used to barter with our husbands for favors or what we call peace. It's communion. Intimacy. Connection. It's holy.

But for many of us, especially those of us who've never engaged in healthy conversations about desire, orgasms or have experienced the pleasures or intimate connections with our partners, we may feel like sex is a burden, a trap, one of those dirty things good girls didn't discuss and hate engaging in.

When we have only been given the traditional "birds and the bees" talks or suffered through nervous conversations with parents who attempt to educate us based on their limited experiences or views, we're left confused, afraid to ask questions, or curious about how to explore further.

If your parents were like mine, the conversation started and ended with, "You better not bring no babies in this house."

It's hard becoming a wife without having a clear understanding of how close connections with our husbands should feel, feeling that fear of not knowing what genuine desire is, or having the urge to explore our husbands' bodies and be open to allowing them to explore ours.

Intimacy shouldn't feel like a chore, a sin, or something that is frowned upon as being dirty or unclean. It's an opportunity to truly connect on a deeper level, an opportunity to experience intimacy in a way where words aren't necessary. Still, the tenderness of touch, when our senses awaken, and our bodies create beautiful music.

Without having this knowledge and complete understanding of the impact, we enter marriage cautious, guarded, and sometimes ashamed.

God didn't give us that spirit of fear—not even in the bedroom.

Unpacking the Myths

Let's clear some things up. Sex, for the wife who loves God, isn't just allowed—it's encouraged. That spark we feel? That longing? That curiosity? Those aren't worldly weaknesses. That's divine wiring.

Somewhere along the way, we were taught to shut down. To fold up our sensuality like a Sunday dress we'd only worn when someone asked for it.

But God never said that. In fact, He created that spark between us and our husband as a gift.

"The two shall become one flesh." —*Ephesians 5:31 (NIV)*

It wasn't a suggestion. It was a blueprint. Oneness—emotionally, spiritually, and yes, physically.

This Is About More Than the Act

Intimacy isn't just the climax—it's the connection. It's the way our husbands look at us after a long day and still see the one they chose. It's the safety we build together. It's the moment our body reminds him he's still wanted, even when words haven't come easily.

And no—this isn't about being some flawless seductress.

This is about leaning in.

- Even when we're tired.
- Even when we feel bloated.
- Even when we haven't shaved our legs.

Because real intimacy is raw. It's the kind where love shows up in a T-shirt and grace.

Pleasure Is Not Just His—It's Ours

Let's be even more real: many women still struggle to believe they're allowed to want to be pleased. That it's okay to not just give—but to receive.

And if we haven't heard this before, listen up: Our pleasure matters. Not as a reward. Not as an afterthought. But as part of the gift.

That doesn't make us "*too much.*" That doesn't make us "*ungodly.*" That makes us human. Married. And free.

Shame Has to Go

So many of us are carrying shame from things that happened before marriage—or the lack of healthy conversation inside of it. And when we bring shame into the bedroom, it doesn't just block our joy—it blocks our healing.

God is not asking us to perform. He's asking us to show up whole. Not perfect. Whole. That means being emotionally open. Spiritually present. Physically willing to be loved and to love back.

"Therefore, there is now no condemnation for those who are in Christ Jesus." —Romans 8:1 (NIV)

So, if we've been feeling like we're not doing it right, or we're not enough, or we don't feel sexy anymore—pause. Breathe. Remember: this was never about comparison. This was never about performance.

Intimacy Is Worship, Too

When we serve our husbands with love and intention—even in the bedroom—we're honoring our vows. We're building trust. We're tending to the vine.

We are not just his wife. We are his safe place. His affirmation. And in that sacred space, our intimacy becomes an offering. One that God can bless.

Give Us Grace

Sometimes, the most healing thing we can do is let ourselves enjoy what we've been given. To drop the rules, the "shoulds," the timelines—and simply show up with curiosity and care.

Try something new. Laugh during it. Hold hands after. Speak life over your body, our bedroom, our bond.

Because when we do? It shifts everything. The fights hit differently. The tension softens faster. The joy becomes contagious.

Reflection Questions:

1. What beliefs about intimacy have you inherited that need healing or replacing?
2. How can you healthily communicate your needs and desires this week?
3. What would it look like to create space for fun, spiritual, healing intimacy with your husband—without pressure but with purpose?

Conclusion

The Real Work Is Sacred.

If you've made it to the end of this book, you've proven something:

You're in this for the long haul.

Not for the fantasy—but for the faithfulness.

Marriage isn't about the happily ever after. It's about the Holy Ever After.

It's about learning to hold on even when the feelings fade, and the flaws show up.

It's about choosing one another when everything inside you says you shouldn't.

I cannot promise that, after reading this, everything will become perfect miraculously.

We all know that this isn't a fairytale. This is real love and real life.

I promise this: if you let God meet you where you are, He will transform everything.

- He will create in you the you that you didn't imagine was possible.
- He'll change the way you see your husband.
- He'll soften the places in your heart that had grown hard.

- He'll rebuild the love that once felt like it was slipping through your fingers.

So, as you close this book, don't close your heart.

Stay open. Stay teachable. Stay honest.

Not just with your husband, yourself, and most importantly, with the God who's holding both of you.

Because of this love?

When built on surrender and strengthened by grace?

It lasts.

Even through the toughest of storms.

Especially through the storms.

Lesson By Lesson Scripture Summary

The scriptures for each lesson was retrieved from:

https://www.biblegateway.com/

Lesson 1:

- *Genesis 2:24* — Marriage as spiritual joining
- *1 Corinthians 13:4–7* — The nature of enduring love.
- *Philippians 1:6* — God will complete what He started.

Lesson 2:

- *1 John 4:18* — Perfect love casts out fear.
- *Proverbs 3:5–6* — Trusting God above our understanding.

Lesson 3:

- *2 Corinthians 10:5* — Taking thoughts captive.
- *1 Corinthians 7:28* — Trouble in marriage is normal.
- *Hebrews 11:1* — Faith in the unseen.

Lesson 4:

- *Romans 8:28* — God uses everything for good.
- *Psalm 147:3* — He heals the brokenhearted.
- *Isaiah 43:2* — God's presence in hardship.

Lesson 5:

- *1 Peter 5:7* — Cast your cares on Him.
- *Ecclesiastes 3:1* — There is a time for everything.

Lesson 6:

- *James 4:6* — God gives grace to the humble.
- *Matthew 11:28–30* — Rest in surrender.
- *Romans 12:2* — Renewing our minds.

Lesson 7:

- *2 Corinthians 6:14* — Do not be unequally yoked.
- *Galatians 6:9* — Do not grow weary in doing good.
- *Proverbs 14:1* — The wise woman builds her house.
- *Ephesians 5:21* — Submit to one another.

Lesson 8:

- *Galatians 6:9* — Perseverance in doing good.
- *Isaiah 40:31* — Renewing strength through the Lord.

Lesson 9:

- *Nehemiah 4:13–14* — Guarding your home.
- *Proverbs 4:23* — Guard your heart.
- *1 Peter 5:8* — Be watchful, the enemy prowls.
- *Ephesians 6:12* — Spiritual warfare is real.

Lesson 10:

- *Mark 3:25* — A house divided cannot stand.

- *Amos 3:3* — Can two walk together unless they agree?

Lesson 11:

- *Proverbs 4:7* — Wisdom is the principal thing.
- *1 Peter 3:7* — Husbands must understand and honor wives.
- *James 1:5* — Ask God for wisdom.

Lesson 12:

- *Hebrews 13:5* — God never leaves us.
- *Psalm 34:18* — God is near to the brokenhearted.
- *Ecclesiastes 4:9–12* — Two are better than one.

Lesson 13:

- *Proverbs 15:1* — A soft answer turns away wrath.
- *Ephesians 4:29* — Speak what builds up.
- *James 1:19* — Be quick to listen, slow to speak.

Lesson 14:

- *Song of Solomon 4:7* — You are altogether beautiful.
- *Psalm 139:14* — Fearfully and wonderfully made.
- *Proverbs 31:25* — She is clothed with strength and dignity.

Lesson 15:

- *Proverbs 24:3–4* — Wisdom builds the house.

- *Romans 12:10* — Be devoted to one another.
- *Philippians 2:3* — Consider others above yourselves.

Lesson 16 (Merged with 25):

- *Ephesians 5:21–25* — Mutual submission and love.
- *Proverbs 3:5–6* — Trust in the Lord for direction.
- *1 Corinthians 13:4* — Love is patient and kind.
- *Psalm 127:1* — Unless the Lord builds the house...

Lesson 17:

- *Ecclesiastes 9:9* — Enjoy life with your spouse.
- *Song of Solomon 1:2* — Let him kiss me.
- *1 Corinthians 7:3–5* — Fulfill marital duty with love.

Lesson 18:

- *2 Corinthians 4:8–9* — Hard-pressed but not crushed.
- *James 1:2–4* — Trials produce perseverance.
- *Romans 5:3–5* — Suffering produces character.

Lesson 19:

- *Proverbs 18:13* — Listen before answering.
- *Job 2:13* — Be present in silence.
- *Ecclesiastes 3:7* — A time to be silent and a time to speak.

Lesson 20:

- *Philippians 4:6–7* — Peace of God guards your heart.
- *Isaiah 26:3* — God keeps in perfect peace.

Lesson 21:

- *Romans 8:28* — God works all things for good.
- *Psalm 127:1* — Unless the Lord builds the house…

Lesson 22:

- *James 1:19–20* — Be slow to anger.
- *Proverbs 29:11* — Fools give full vent to rage.
- *Ephesians 4:26* — Don't let the sun go down on anger.

Lesson 23:

- *Matthew 11:28–30* — Come to me, I will give you rest.
- *Isaiah 40:29–31* — He gives strength to the weary.
- *Philippians 4:13* — I can do all things through Christ.

Lesson 24:

- *1 Samuel 16:7* — God looks at the heart.
- *Genesis 2:25* — They were both naked and felt no shame.
- *1 Corinthians 6:19–20* — Your body is a temple.

About The Author

Ce'ce Perez

Ce'ce Perez is a native Floridian, seasoned writer, editor, and book consultant with advanced degrees in Literature and Creative Writing. With a lifelong passion for storytelling and over a decade of experience in publishing, she has worked for multiple publishing houses, edited for others, and helped aspiring authors bring their work to life.

She is the founder of **Writer's Wisdom**, a platform dedicated to equipping writers with the tools, strategy, and encouragement needed to write, refine, and share their stories with purpose. As the voice behind *Ce'ce's Book Review*, she's also offered insightful reviews that support new and emerging authors across genres.

Whether crafting her own projects or guiding others through theirs, Ce'ce brings clarity, faith, and creativity to everything she touches— writing for women and men alike who are ready to embrace their voice and calling.

www.ingramcontent.com/pod-product-compliance
Lightning Source LLC
Chambersburg PA
CBHW060505030426
42337CB00015B/1749